Physical Characteristics of the Australian Terrier

(from the American Kennel Club breed standard)

Body: Of sturdy structure with ribs well-sprung but not rounded.

Topline: Level and firm.

Loin: Strong and fairly short with slight tuck-up.

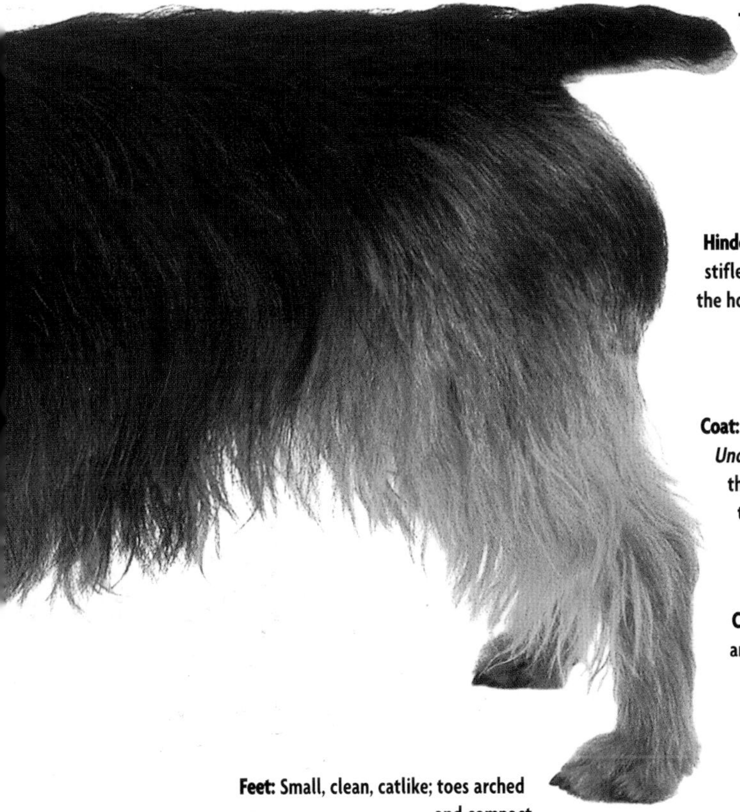

Tail: Docked in balance with the overall dog leaving slightly less than one half.

Hindquarters: Strong; legs well angulated at the stifles and hocks, short and perpendicular from the hocks to the ground.

Coat: *Outer Coat*—Harsh and straight. *Undercoat*—Short and soft. *Furnishings*—Softer than body coat. *Topknot*—Of finer and softer texture than the rest of the coat.

Colors: Blue and tan, solid sandy and solid red.

Feet: Small, clean, catlike; toes arched and compact.

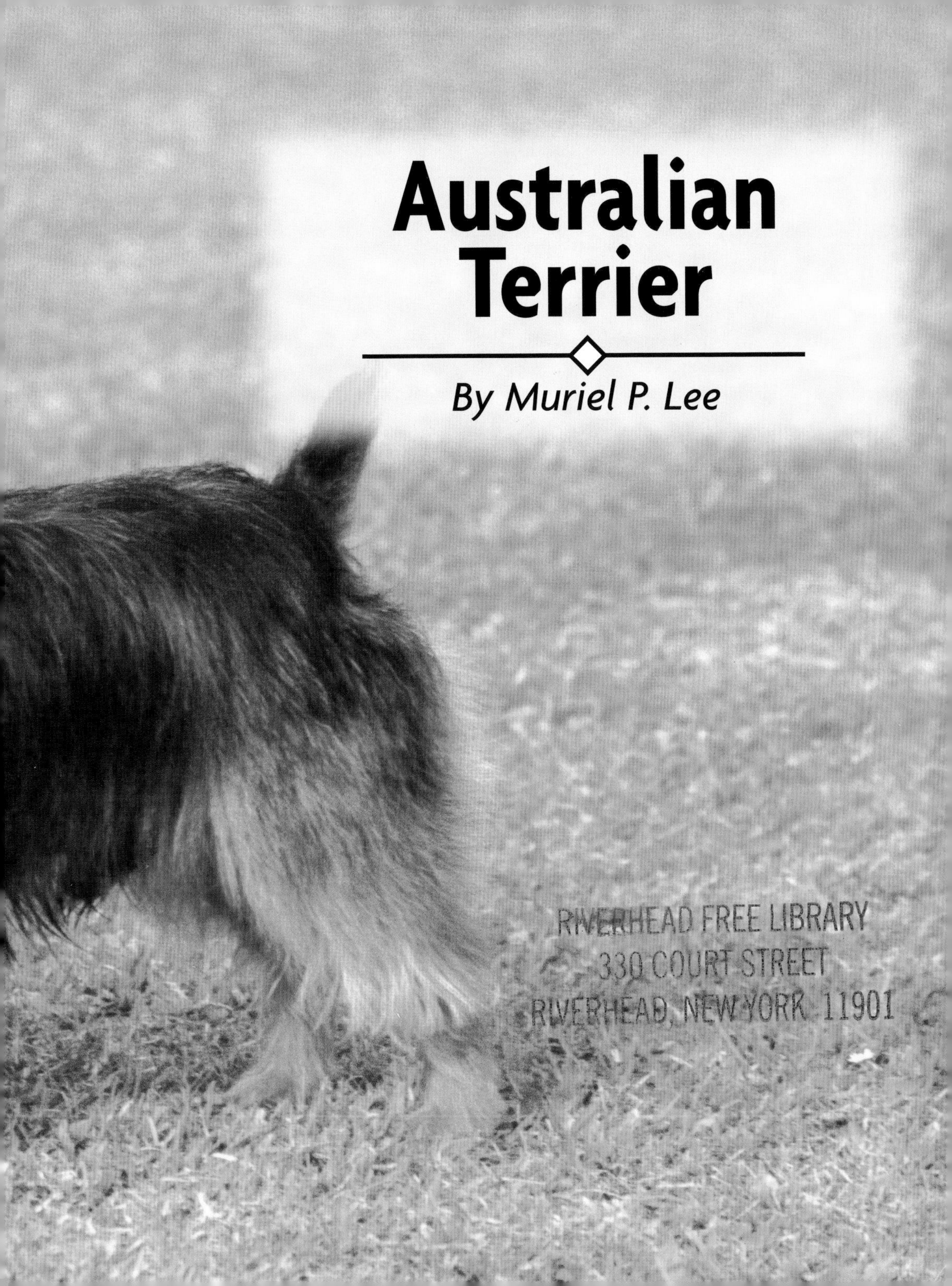

Australian Terrier

By Muriel P. Lee

Contents

KENNEL CLUB BOOKS: **AUSTRALIAN TERRIER**

ISBN: 1-59378-290-X

308 Main Street, Allenhurst, New Jersey 07711 USA

Cover Design Patented: US 6,435,559 B2 • Printed in South Korea

10 9 8 7 6 5 4 3 2 1

Photography by

Paulette Braun, T.J. Calhoun, Alan & Sandy Carey, Carolina Biological Supply, Isabelle Français, Carol Ann Johnson, Bill Jonas, Dr. Dennis Kunkel, Tam C. Nguyen, Phototake, Jean Claude Revy, Alice Roche, Karen Taylor, Michael Trafford, Alice van Kempen and Mike & Sue Young.

Illustrations by Patricia Peters.

The publisher wishes to thank all of the owners whose dogs are featured in this book, including Vicki Benz, Richard & Ann Marie Hunter, Esther C. Krom, Alice & Neal Roche, Alexis Samarotta, Karen A. Ucci, Ida Ellen Weinstock and Alice Ann Wight.

Hailing from sunny Australia, this friendly chap is pleased to make your acquaintance.

HISTORY OF THE AUSTRALIAN TERRIER

The Australian Terrier is a small, confident, robust little dog that hails from Australia. He owes his beginnings to the early settlers of the country who were looking for a courageous, tough dog that was game and also an excellent ratter. Although he now is most often a loyal companion for his family, his original terrier instincts have not been lost, and he will be equally at home on a country estate, in a suburban home or in a city apartment.

This book will give you the history, description and breed standard of the Australian Terrier. You will also learn about puppy care, training and the health of the breed. From the photographs, you will meet the breed face-to-face and see that this terrier is a real charmer and a wonderful companion dog.

This may not be the dog for everyone, as terriers are active, busy dogs and the Australian Terrier is no exception. However, if you like a plucky dog, one that fits easily into city or country life, this may be just the dog for you. Frederick David wrote, "No one who has owned an Australian Terrier ever desires to own any other kind of dog."

ORIGIN AND ESTABLISHMENT

The Australian Terrier, although a relative youngster to the American pure-bred fancy, being recognized by the AKC in 1960, was registered in England in the 1930s and has been known in Australia since the 19th century. At the present time, around 70% of Australian families have dogs, and thousands compete every week in dog shows, obedience competitions and agility trials. This is a country where, indeed, the dog not only is necessary for work but also is a beloved pet and companion, a true part of the family.

Australia has developed several breeds. The dingo, the native dog, was there to greet the British when they arrived in the country in the early 1800s, bringing their British dogs with them. Over time, Australians developed five breeds: the Australian Cattle

SILKY IN SYDNEY

MacArthur Little was an early breeder of the Silky Terrier, which was called the Sydney Terrier when he moved his kennel to Sydney. The Silky Terrier is a mixture of the Australian Terrier and the Yorkshire Terrier, and is in the Toy Group with the Yorkie rather than in the Terrier Group with the Aussie. The Silky is a friendly, independent, smart, energetic and affectionate dog, bred to be a household pet.

Dog, the Australian Kelpie, the Stumpy Tail Cattle Dog, the Silky Terrier (at one time called the Sydney Terrier and now officially known in its homeland as the Australian Silky Terrier) and the Australian Terrier. The Cattle Dog and Kelpie were developed to handle the sheep and cattle on the vast farming lands, but a small, tough terrier was needed to be used against rats, vermin and snakes in order to make the land more habitable.

The Australian Terrier belongs to the group of dogs described as terriers, from the Latin word *terra*, meaning "earth." The terrier is a dog that has been bred to work beneath the ground to drive out small and large vermin, rodents and other animals that can be nuisances to country living.

Nearly all of the dogs in the Terrier Group originated in the British Isles, with the exception of the Australian Terrier and the Cesky Terrier. Although these two breeds do not hail from the British Isles, they both were developed from British dogs: the Cesky from an original cross of the Scottish Terrier and the Sealyham Terrier, and the Australian Terrier from a series of crosses of various terrier breeds.

The terrier background is obscure, but what was certain in the 1700s and early 1800s was that there was no definite breed of terrier; rather, there were dogs that were bred to go to ground with courage and conviction. In 1735, the *Sportsman's Dictionary* described the terrier as a kind of hound, used only or chiefly for hunting the fox or badger. "He creeps into the ground and then nips and bites the fox and badger, either by tearing them in pieces with his teeth, or else hauling them and pulling them by force out of their lurking holes."

Those who were unable to do the job were destroyed; dogs were not considered worthy "unless they were fit and game for the purpose." Those who could do the proper work were bred to one another with little regard for type. Those who bred and kept dogs had specific purposes for their particular breeds; for example, long legs for speed, short legs for going to ground and double coats for protection against the elements.

Moreover, all terriers have powerful teeth.

Many of the terrier breeds were derived from a similar ancestor and, as recently as the mid 1800s, the terriers fell roughly into two basic categories: the rough-coated, short-legged dogs that tended to come from Scotland, and the longer-legged, smooth-coated dogs that were bred in England. The terriers, although they may differ in type, all have the same basic character, being game dogs who go after vermin or other larger animals.

In the early 1800s, in the island state of Tasmania, the settlers were breeding broken-coated terriers that weighed from 7 to 10 pounds and were blue in body color, with tan legs and faces. These dogs were prized for hearing so keenly that they could easily detect any strangers approaching the farmstead. It is assumed that the roots of these dogs went back to the dog now known as the Yorkshire Terrier; possibly this breed could be a common ancestor of both the Australian Terrier and the Silky Terrier.

In time, breeders were trying to develop a larger, tougher blue and tan terrier, working particularly to establish a breed of dog that could control vermin, snakes, rabbits and any other small game that were destructive to farm life in the outbacks.

The broken-haired dogs were crossed with Cairn Terriers to give a harsh and weatherproof coat. The old-time Scotch Terrier was used not only for his coat but also for the conformation of his head. The Dandie Dinmont Terrier added the soft top-knot, and the prick-eared Skye Terrier gave the ear carriage and the length of body. A small Irish Terrier could also have been used, and the Manchester Terrier and Yorkshire Terrier were both used to enrich the coat color.

Mr. Eric Dart, a noted Australian Terrier breeder who perfected the red and sandy colors in the breed, wrote to an English

CANIS LUPUS

"Grandma, what big teeth you have!" The gray wolf, a familiar figure in fairy tales and legends, has had its reputation tarnished and its population pummeled over the centuries. Yet it is the descendants of this much-feared creature to which we open our homes and hearts. Our beloved dog, *Canis domesticus*, derives directly from the gray wolf, a highly social canine that lives in elaborately structured packs. In the wild, the gray wolf can range from 60 to 175 pounds, standing between 25 and 40 inches in height.

IN THE MIX

The Australian Terrier was being bred to the Cairn Terrier as late as the 1940s in order to improve coat texture and for the Cairn's terrier character. In the early years of breed development, on occasion the Australian Terrier, Silky Terrier and Yorkshire Terrier could all come from the same litter.

breeder in the 1930s about the difficulties of stabilizing the breed on a continent as large as Australia. Added to the great distances between breeders, there were also differing views in the various states as to just what an Aussie should look like. He wrote, "It is difficult to place much reliance in the claims made by fanciers concerning the merits of the breed in by-gone years, as it is impossible to trace any dog or bitch of outstanding merit in any existing pedigrees who might be said to have had a beneficial influence on the breed; nor can we find any kennel or strain predominatory in past records. In all probability, the Australian Terrier at the time the Standard was drawn

The Yorkshire Terrier, shown here in its modern-day incarnation, was used to enrich the Australian Terrier's color.

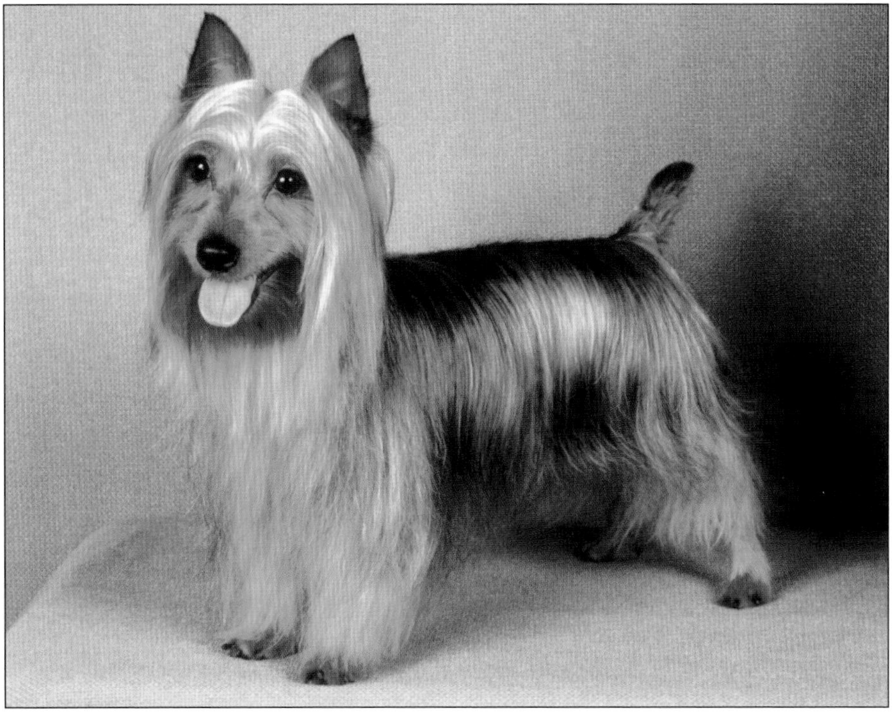

The Silky Terrier, shown here, is a mixture of Australian Terrier and Yorkshire Terrier breeding. The Silky is much smaller than the Aussie and thus is classified as a toy breed like the Yorkie. It also shares its silky coat with the Yorkie, while the Aussie has a broken, or harsh, coat.

up, forty odd years ago, was a very badly put together little dog."

In 1872 in Melbourne, the Australian dogs were shown for the first time in the "Broken-Coated Terrier" class. By 1880 they were classified as "Blue and Tans," by 1882 they were "Toys" and by 1884 they were shown as "Australian Rough-Coated Terriers." This was also the first year that sandy-colored dogs were shown with the blue and tan dogs.

In 1889, the Australian Rough Coated Terrier Club was formed in Melbourne; by 1901 the club had 50 members. Indeed, the breed was often drawing the largest numbers of entries at shows at the turn of the 19th century.

The Aussies were indeed popular. The well-known writer Freeman Lloyd wrote in 1901, "There are large classes of Australian Terriers. They are

AUSSIE OR SILKY?

In 1935, Will Judy noted, "The ruling of the New South Wales (Australia) Club for one breed and one standard has not been adopted universally and so the confusion [between the Sydney Silky and the Aussie] continues with little credit to the breeders in Australia."

bigger than Yorkies and should be short and harsh in coat, but they do not seem particularly attractive dogs. These dogs are, however, very plentiful, possess 'type' and are game and excellent ratters. If one cares to take a stroll on the esplanade at St. Kilda, the suburban and seaside resort of Melbourne, on a Sunday, he may observe as many as forty to fifty following enjoyment seekers. From this one can easily see they are in great requisition as companions, and I have noticed many carried as lapdogs by ladies in carriages."

By 1896 a breed standard was written, giving breeders a picture of what the breed should look like and what they should try to achieve in their breeding programs. By 1897 fanciers of the Australian Terriers and the Silky Terriers formed a club, but this was short-lived, with the Silky Terrier and Yorkshire Terrier people forming their own club. It was not until the 1940s that a club was formed for the Australian Terrier, with W. A. Wheatland as president.

The original breed standard was written in 1896, revised in 1947 and later changed to some degree in 1962. In 1964 Mr. Wheatland wrote the book *The Australian Terrier and the Australian Silky Terrier*, which lists the three different standards. The original standard allowed either prick or drop ears, but this was amended in the 1920s, allowing erect ears only.

SEEING RED

During the 1880s, the red color was introduced to the breed, possibly from a number of red terriers that were being imported into Australia from England. The Irish Terriers, Border Terriers and Norwich Terriers could have been imported, in addition to the red and sandy Cairns. Any of these could have been responsible for adding the red color to the previously blue and tan broken-haired dog. The red and sandies can still have difficulty being accepted in the show ring.

THE AUSSIE GOES GLOBAL

In 1906, Australian Terriers were being exported to England, and a Mr. Milburn exhibited a few at The Kennel Club show. A few more were shown in 1907, but it was not

Today the Australian Terrier is an active, friendly house pet that still retains its natural ratting instincts.

Australian Terriers were exported to the USA via returning soldiers from World War II. Despite growing interest in the breed, it was not recognized by the American Kennel Club until 1960.

until after World War I that the breed established a small following in Britain. In the early 1920s Lady Stradbroke, whose husband had been the Governor of Victoria, brought a number of dogs to England with her. Sir Claude and Lady Alexander, well-known Skye Terrier breeders, also became interested in the breed. In 1934 the Duke of Gloucester brought a pair of Aussies home with him and the breed became better known in the British Isles. However, with the advent of World War II, the breed fell upon hard times—as many breeds did—but by 1945 the breed was on the upswing again.

Australian Terriers were brought to America after World War II, being carried over by many American soldiers who found the dog to be a most pleasing sort, in addition to being small and easy to carry. However, the breed was not registrable with the American Kennel Club at that time; there was no national club and no effort was made to see that the breed had a following.

Mrs. E. Williams of Willelva Kennels was a well-known breeder in Australia. Her first dog, purchased from Baroldy Kennels in 1949, was Baroldy Terry-Boy. He became a well-known Aussie champion, winning many Bests of Breed at the largest of shows, in addition to being the first Aussie in New South Wales to win a Group. Mrs. Williams later purchased Baroldy Topsy who, when bred to Terry-Boy, produced some excellent red litters. In 1956, Mrs. Williams sold a blue and tan Aussie to Mrs. Milton Fox of Pleasant Pastures Kennels in Point Pleasant, New Jersey.

Mrs. Fox, a native of New Zealand, had owned Australian Terriers as a youngster. In the 1950s she imported a few Aussies from England and, in 1956, she bought the blue and tan dog Willelva William, a son of Terry-Boy, from Mrs. Williams. Mrs. Fox gave her heart to the breed and became the most ardent supporter of the Australian Terrier for her lifetime. She was a tireless worker for breed acceptance by the American Kennel Club. She entered the

PURE-BRED PURPOSE

Given the vast range of the world's 400 or so pure breeds of dog, it's fair to say that domestic dogs are the most versatile animal in the kingdom. From the tiny 1-pound lap dog to the 200-pound guard dog, dogs have adapted to every need and whim of their human masters. Humans have selectively bred dogs to alter physical attributes like size, color, leg length, mass and skull diameter in order to suit our own needs and fancies. Dogs serve humans not only as companions and guardians but also as hunters, exterminators, shepherds, rescuers, messengers, warriors, babysitters and more!

Miscellaneous Classes as well as obedience competition with her dogs. She later imported Willelva Wanderer, who became the first Aussie to earn his Companion Dog title in obedience and was the sire of the first American Australian Terrier champion. It was due to Mrs. Fox and her Pleasant Pastures Kennels that the breed was recognized by the American Kennel Club in 1960.

The Australian Terrier was entered in the Miscellaneous Class at Westminster in 1958 with an entry of nine. In 1959, due to Mrs. Fox's super-human efforts, the entry was increased to 44. In 1960, it had reached the phenomenal number of 58 entries. The breed was recognized by the AKC in 1960 and was the 114th breed to be accepted by the organization. The Australian Terrier Club of America (ATCA) was founded in 1957, but it did not become a member club of the AKC until 1977. Today the club has over 200 members.

Mrs. Fox owned, bred and imported numerous dogs from Australia and England, making up over 200 champions and many Group winners. Her greatest dog,

The Australian Terrier is a long, low, sturdy breed that has retained moderate popularity since the early 1900s.

Ch. Tinee Town Talkbac, "Joey," sired 46 AKC champions, won 4 all-breed Bests in Show and had 29 Group Ones.

The January 26, 1976 issue of *The New Yorker* magazine featured an extensive article about Mrs. Fox, her dogs and her journey with the dogs and helpers to the Westminster Kennel Club show. She was certainly a prominent Australian Terrier breeder as well as a character in her own right. In 1994 the Australian Terrier Club of America honored Mrs. Fox with the title of Lifetime Patroness of the ATCA for her lifetime work for the breed. In 1997, she was honored for 50 years as a breeder, exhibitor and prominent club member.

Aussies continue to be fairly popular in America; registrations are consistently well over 400 per year. Across the Atlantic, entries at a recent Crufts show (the largest show in the UK) were 40, placing the Aussie higher in popularity than many other terrier breeds in the UK, but with a much smaller number of entries than the larger terriers.

The breed is still very popular in Australia with many prominent breeders, both in the past and at the present time. Tinee Town Kennels bred Ch. Tinee Town Talktime, who was Best in Show at the Sydney Royal Show in 1973. Aust. and Am. Ch. Tinee Town Talkbac was Best in Show several times in Australia before being sent to Mrs. Fox in the United States. Several other prominent kennels are Sevenoaks, Elmore, Taralee and Taggalong.

Aussies are known and loved throughout the world. Mrs. Fox wrote, "For a true lover of dogs with prime devotion to Terriers, it is impossible not to have deep affection for the whole Terrier Group. However, once acquainted with Aussies, one's admiration remains steadfast. The unbounding devotion from puppyhood, the original manner of doing things, almost a sense of humor, the fact of their being so easy to care for, added to their protective, responsive natures, make them courageous companions beyond compare."

TOP DOGS

An excerpt from *The New Yorker* magazine, January 26, 1976: "Mrs. Fox cuts in firmly to say that she knows right after it's born when one of her Australian Terriers is going to be a top dog. 'Or I think I do...of course, they may turn out differently when you start to show them. But once you've begun to take them into the ring, it's easy to tell. The best dogs practically beg you to show them off. Joey can't wait to get into the ring.' 'That's true,' Mrs Tompkins says. 'They're like Shirley Temple. When Shirley Temple's mother said, "Sparkle!" she sparkled. That's the way top dogs are. That's what divides the star from the chorus'."

CHARACTERISTICS OF THE
AUSTRALIAN TERRIER

HEART-HEALTHY

In this modern age of ever-improving cardio-care, no doctor or scientist can dispute the advantages of owning a dog to lower a person's risk of heart disease. Studies have proven that petting a dog, walking a dog and grooming a dog all show positive results toward lowering your blood pressure. The simple routine of exercising your dog—going outside with the dog and walking, jogging or playing catch—is heart-healthy in and of itself. If you are normally less active than your physician thinks you should be, adopting a dog may be a smart option to improve your own quality of life as well as that of another creature.

The Australian Terrier is a versatile dog, and a great house dog and companion. If you like to work with your dog, you will find the Aussie to be a happy and willing participant in whatever area you choose, be it obedience work, agility, therapy, flyball and, of course, best of all, going-to-ground activities. This is a smart little dog that likes to please, to keep busy and to be challenged. Give him any job that requires a bit of brain activity on his part and he will be as pleased as punch. Of course, because of his intelligence, it is best to establish very early on who is the head of the household and, thus, basic obedience lessons are essential.

The Aussie has an air of self-assurance and he is inquisitive about everything that happens in his vicinity. He has keen hearing and excellent eyesight, and he makes an outstanding watchdog. He can adapt to any climate with his double waterproof coat that sheds very little. He will accept full responsibility for the household. He will like the entire family, but he is likely to attach himself to one particular family member. He is an active dog and needs his regular daily romps. It is said that he is "long enough on leg not to collect much mud and small enough to fit into any home." All in all, this is a delightful little dog to become part of your household.

HAVE SOME FUN!

Australian Terrier owners should have fun with their dogs! Not only will Aussies thrive on organized activities, they also love to be a part of the family, going for rides in the car, fetching balls (sometimes for hours on end, to their owners' dismay) and helping in the kitchen by keeping the floor clean...and then cuddling up for a snooze on the bed when day is done.

Australian Terriers are curious and alert little explorers, thoroughly enjoying time outdoors.

If you are a first-time dog owner, you must be aware of your responsibility toward your new friend. You must keep your dog either on a leash or in your fenced yard. Your Aussie, if loose and trotting along at your side, will spot a squirrel and, instinctively, he will dart across the street, oblivious of the traffic. This is why some rudimentary obedience training is necessary so that your pal will sit when asked to, come when called and, in general, act like a little gentleman. Training is necessary for a dog's safety, but it is never advisable to let a dog loose in an unfenced area.

Aussies, as with other terriers, can be challenging in the obedience ring. Terriers are not easy breeds to work with in obedience, as with their intelligence and independent spirits they can sometimes be more trying to train than had been anticipated. You will see Golden Retrievers,

Although curious and active, the Australian Terrier enjoys downtime, too, especially when sharing a cuddle with his favorite person.

Poodles and Miniature Schnauzers in abundance in obedience classes, as these are breeds with which it is easy to work. Not only are they intelligent but, more importantly, they have a willingness to please their masters.

Terriers are easily distracted and busy, but the Aussie is an intelligent dog and he does respond to training. Of course, when training a smart and independent dog, the handler will often learn humility while the dog is learning his sits and stays. The Aussie is a quick, alert and intelligent dog, and he likes his owner to be his equal.

All in all, the Australian Terrier is amiable and affectionate, making an enjoyable companion and loyal friend for almost everyone. He has a particular fondness for children and senior citizens, and he is especially good with the handicapped, making him a great pet for those with special needs or a well-qualified candidate for therapy work. Add to this his adaptability to climate and living environment, and you have a good-tempered, well-rounded, conveniently sized dog, packed with personality and love to give to the owner who has the time to devote to his dog's training and care.

Australian Terriers are very healthy dogs, as are most terriers, and there are few health problems in the breed. Do remember to buy your puppy from a reputable breeder and ask the breeder if he has any health problems in his line. Following are some problems that can affect Australian Terriers.

Legge-Calve-Perthes disease (Perthes): This is a bone-related disease that can affect short-legged terriers (primarily those from Scotland) as well as humans. This is not a hereditary disease; it is thought to be caused by an injury or possibly a nutritional

LIFE WITH A TERRIER

Brian Commons wrote, "Terriers, created to hunt down and kill vermin, should all be sold with their own leather jackets. They are often feisty, lively, self-assured. You live with terriers, you do not own them."

problem. The disease appears between four and ten months of age and is very painful. The dog will limp on one or both rear legs, and eventually the leg muscles become wasted. There are some treatments for Perthes, and these should be discussed with your veterinarian.

Luxated kneecaps (or patellar luxation): In this condition the patella, or kneecap, deviates to the inside of the leg so that the muscles of the leg responsible for straightening the knee are no longer in alignment. This might result in some lameness or complete non-use of the leg. Conditions that cause this problem are a shallow groove, weak ligaments and/or misalignment of the tendons and muscles that straighten the knee joint. The patella can then slip either inward or outward. Your veterinarian should be contacted if you suspect that your dog has this problem, and the vet will manipulate the stifle joint to see if he can push the kneecap in or out of position. Your vet should determine if your dog is a candidate for

DELTA SOCIETY

The human-animal bond propels the work of the Delta Society, striving to improve the lives of people and animals. The Pet Partners Program proves that the lives of people and dogs are inextricably linked. The Pet Partners Program, a national registry, trains and screens volunteers for pet therapy in hospices, nursing homes, schools and rehabilitation centers. Dog-and-handler teams of Pet Partners volunteer in all 50 states, with nearly 7,000 teams making visits annually. About 900,000 patients, residents and students receive assistance each year. If you and your dog are interested in becoming Pet Partners, contact the Delta Society online at www.deltasociety.org.

A well-bred, well-cared-for Australian Terrier will be a healthy, hardy dog and a part of the family for well over a decade.

THE AGE OF ROBO-DOG

Studies at the Center for the Human-Animal Bond show that children who interact with pets benefit physiologically, socially and educationally. Dogs, in particular, increase children's learning capacities and expand their abilities to function in social situations. Families with young children commonly add canines to their homes.

Enter Robo-dog. Efforts to create a robotic canine companion are fast underway, and there have been some interesting results. It is the hope of scientists that the interaction between robotic dogs and children will shed light on the physical, mental, moral and social concepts of such relationships. Robotic dogs offer many advantages over real dogs—they don't require food or water and never have accidents indoors. Even so, Robo-dogs will never take the place of real dogs—even George Jetson's futuristic family included Astro, a real-live dog! It is curious that 21st-century humans would invest so much money and energy into inventing robots to do for us what dogs have been doing for centuries for nothing more than a pat on the head and a bowl of food.

surgery and if this will be an option for him.

Although these health problems may seem daunting, the Aussie is considered to be a very healthy breed. The problems mentioned exist in the breed and a buyer should be aware of them. However, these diseases are rare, so do not let them discourage you from adding an Aussie to your family. Also, do realize that if the breeder of your puppy is reputable and aware of these problems, he

will be doing his utmost to keep them out of his line.

Williams Haynes wrote in 1925, "The terrier is a 'lucky devil' for his dogs do not, as a rule, spend a great deal of time in hospital. All members of the terrier family, from the giant of the race, the Airedale, way down to little Scottie, owe a big debt to Nature for having blessed them with remarkably robust constitutions. Even when really sick, they make wonderfully rapid recoveries."

Healthwise, Australian Terriers are naturally robust and generally free of diseases and infirmities, a characteristic they share with most other terriers.

BREED STANDARD FOR THE AUSTRALIAN TERRIER

As breeders started exhibiting at dog shows, it was realized that there must be more uniformity within the breed, i.e., all puppies in a litter should be of the same type as well as being of the same type as their sire and dam. Each breed approved by the American Kennel Club has a breed standard, which gives the reader a mental picture of what a dog of each particular breed should look like. All reputable breeders strive to produce animals that will meet the requirements of the standard.

Many breeds were developed for a specific purpose, i.e., hunting, retrieving, going to ground, coursing, guarding, herding or working. The Aussie, like most terriers, were bred to go to ground and to pursue vermin. In addition to having dogs that look like proper Australian Terriers, the standard assures that the Aussie will have the personality, disposition, intelligence and abilities that are required in the breed.

Standards were originally written by fanciers who had a love and a concern for the breed. They knew that the essential characteristics of the Australian Terrier were unlike those of any other breed and that care must be taken that these characteristics were maintained through the generations. As time progressed and breeders became more aware that certain areas of the dog needed a better description or more definition, breeders would meet together and work out a new standard. However, standards for any breed are never changed on a whim, and serious study and exchange between breeders take place before any revision is considered.

According to the breed standard, the Australian Terrier has a harsh, straight outer coat and a keen and intelligent expression.

THE AMERICAN KENNEL CLUB STANDARD FOR THE AUSTRALIAN TERRIER

General Appearance: A small, sturdy, medium-boned working terrier, rather long in proportion to height with pricked ears and docked tail. Blue and tan, solid sandy or solid red in color, with harsh-textured outer coat, a distinctive ruff and apron, and a soft, silky topknot. As befits their heritage as versatile workers, Australian Terriers are sound and free moving with good reach and drive. Their expression keen and intelligent; their manner spirited and self-assured.

The following description is that of the ideal Australian Terrier. Any deviation from this description must be penalized to the extent of the deviation.

Size, Proportion, Substance: *Size*—Height 10–11 inches at the withers. Deviation in either direction is to be discouraged. *Proportion*—The body is long in proportion to the height of the dog. The length of back from withers to the front of the tail is approximately 1–1½ inches longer than from withers to the ground. *Substance*—Good working condition, medium bone, correct body proportions, symmetry and balance determine proper weight.

Long in proportion and sturdy describe the well-bred typical Australian Terrier.

Head: The head is long and strong. The length of the muzzle is equal to the length of the skull. *Expression*—Keen and intelligent. *Eyes*—Small, dark brown to black (the darker the better), keen in expression, set well apart. Rims are black, oval in shape. *Faults:* Light-colored or protruding eyes. *Ears*—Small, erect and pointed; set high on the skull yet well apart, carried erect without any tendency to flare obliquely off the skull. *Skull*—Viewed from the front or side is long and flat, slightly longer than it is wide and full between the eyes, with slight but definite stop. *Muzzle*—Strong and powerful with slight fill under the eyes. The jaws are powerful. *Nose*—Black. A desirable breed characteristic is an inverted V-shaped area free of hair extending from the nose up the bridge of the muzzle, varying in length in the mature dog. *Lips*—Tight and dark brown- or black-rimmed. *Bite*—Scissors with teeth of good size.

Neck, Topline, Body: *Neck*—Long, slightly arched and strong, blending smoothly into well laid back shoulders. *Topline*—Level and firm. *Body*—The body is of sturdy structure with ribs well-sprung but not rounded, forming a chest reaching slightly below the elbows with a distinct keel. The loin is strong and fairly short with slight tuck-up. *Faults:* Cobbiness, too long in loin. *Tail*—Set on high and carried erect at a twelve to one o'clock position, docked in balance with the overall dog leaving slightly

Dog shows revolve around the breed standard and the judge's interpretation of it. The dog that most closely adheres to the standard, in the judge's opinion, is the dog that takes home the top awards.

less than one half, a good handhold when mature.

Forequarters: *Shoulders*—Long blades, well laid back with only slight space between the shoulder blades at the withers. The length of the upper arm is comparable to the length of the shoulder blade. The angle between the shoulder and the upper arm is 90 degrees. *Faults:* Straight, loose and loaded shoulders. *Elbows*—Close to the chest. *Forelegs*—Straight, parallel when viewed from the front; the bone is round and medium in size. They should be set well under the body, with definite body overhang (keel) before them when viewed from the side. *Pasterns*—Strong, with only slight slope. *Fault*: Down on pasterns. *Dewclaws*—Removed. *Feet*—Small, clean, catlike; toes arched and compact, nicely padded turning neither inward nor outward. *Nails*—Short, black and strong.

The Australian Terrier ideally possesses a scissors bite with good-sized teeth.

MEETING THE IDEAL

The American Kennel Club defines a standard as: "A description of the ideal dog of each recognized breed, to serve as an ideal against which dogs are judged at shows." This "blueprint" is drawn up by the breed's recognized parent club, approved by a majority of its membership and then submitted to the AKC for approval.

The AKC states that "An understanding of any breed must begin with its standard. This applies to all dogs, not just those intended for showing." The picture that the standard draws of the dog's type, gait, temperament and structure is the guiding image used by breeders as they plan their programs.

Hindquarters: Strong; legs well angulated at the stifles and hocks, short and perpendicular from the hocks to the ground. Upper and lower thighs are well muscled. Viewed from behind the rear legs are straight from the hip joints to the ground and in the same plane as the forelegs. *Faults:* Lack of muscular development or excessive muscularity. *Feet*—(See under Forequarters.)

Coat: *Outer Coat*—Harsh and straight; 2½ inches all over the body except the tail, pasterns, rear legs from the hocks down and the feet which are kept free of long hair. Hair on the ears is kept very short. *Undercoat*—Short and soft. *Furnishings*—Softer than body coat. The neck is well furnished with hair, which forms a protective ruff blending into the apron. The forelegs are slightly feathered to the pasterns. *Topknot*—Covering only the top of the skull; of finer and softer texture than the rest of the coat.

Color and Markings: *Colors:* Blue and tan, solid sandy and solid red. *Blue and tan*—Blue: dark blue, steel-blue, dark gray-blue or silver-blue. In silver-blues, each hair carries blue and silver alternating with the darker color at the tips. Tan markings (not sandy or red),

Although possessing an overall rugged look, today's Aussie is just as happy at home as he is in the outback. His friendly, obedient personality and compact size make him a wonderful house pet for active owners.

as rich as possible, on face, ears, underbody, lower legs and feet, and around vent. The richer the color and more clearly defined the better. *Topknot*—Silver or a lighter shade than head color. *Sandy or Red*—Any shade of solid sandy or solid red, the clearer the better. *Topknot*—Silver or a lighter shade of body coat. *Faults:* All black body coat in the adult dog. Tan smut in the blue portion of the coat, or dark smut in sandy/red coated dogs. In any color, white markings on chest or feet are to be penalized.

Whether a show dog or a house pet, the Australian Terrier appears as a natural working dog, wholly unexaggerated and untrimmed.

Gait: As seen from the front and from the rear, the legs are straight from the shoulder and hip joints to the pads, and move in planes parallel to the centerline of travel. The rear legs move in the same planes as the front legs. As the dog moves at a faster trot, the front and rear legs and feet may tend to converge toward the centerline of travel, but the legs remain straight even as they flex or extend. Viewed from the side, the legs move in a ground-covering stride. The rear feet should meet the ground in the same prints as left by the front feet, with no gap between them. Topline remains firm and level, without bounce.

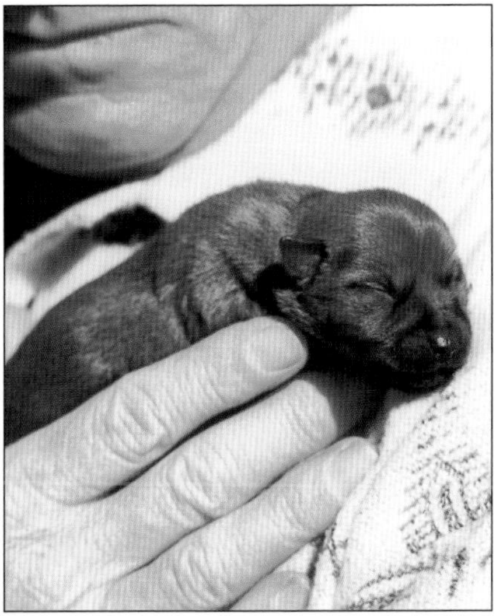

It is impossible to tell what potential a newborn puppy possesses, but breeders do their best to produce good health, good temperament and good type in every litter and pup.

Temperament: The Australian Terrier is spirited, alert, courageous and self-confident, with the natural aggressiveness of a ratter and hedge hunter; as a companion, friendly and affectionate. *Faults:* Shyness or aggressiveness toward people.

Approved August 9, 1988

AUSTRALIAN TERRIER

WHERE TO BEGIN?

If you are convinced that the Australian Terrier is the ideal dog for you, it's time to learn about where to find a puppy and what to look for. Locating a litter of Australian Terriers should not present a problem, but it will require a bit of research. You should inquire about breeders who enjoy good reputations in the breed. You are looking for an established breeder with outstanding dog ethics and a strong commitment to the breed. New owners should have as many questions as they have doubts. An established breeder is indeed the one to answer your four million questions and make you comfortable with your choice of the Australian Terrier. An established breeder will sell you a puppy at a fair price if, and only if, the breeder determines that you are a suitably, worthy owner of his dogs. An established breeder can be relied upon for advice, at any reasonable time of the day. A reputable breeder often will accept a

SELECTING FROM THE LITTER

Before you visit a litter of puppies, promise yourself that you won't fall for the first pretty face you see! Decide on your goals for your puppy—show prospect, therapy dog, obedience competitor, family companion—and then look for a puppy who displays the appropriate qualities. In most litters, there is an Alpha pup (the bossy puppy), and occasionally a shy fellow who is less confident, with the rest of the litter falling somewhere in the middle. "Middle-of-the-roaders" are safe bets for most families and novice competitors.

puppy back with no penalty to you should you decide that this is not the right dog for you.

When choosing a breeder, reputation is much more important than convenience of location. Do not be overly impressed by breeders who run brag advertisements in the canine publications about their stupendous champions. The real quality breeders are quiet and unassuming. You hear about them at dog shows and trials, by word of mouth. You may be well advised to avoid the novice who may live nearby. The novice breeder, trying so hard to get rid of that first litter of puppies, is more than accommodating and anxious to sell you one. That breeder will charge you as much as any established breeder. The novice breeder isn't going to interrogate you and your family about your intentions with the puppy, the environment and training you can provide, etc. That breeder will be nowhere to be found when your poorly bred, badly adjusted four-pawed monster starts to growl and spit up at midnight or pick fights with the family cat!

The breeder begins early socialization with very young pups by gently petting and handling them.

THE FAMILY TREE

Your puppy's pedigree is his family tree. Just as a child may resemble his parents and grandparents, so too will a puppy reflect the qualities, good and bad, of his ancestors, especially those in the first two generations. Therefore it's important to know as much as possible about a puppy's immediate relatives. Reputable and experienced breeders should be able to explain the pedigree and why they chose to breed from the particular dogs they used.

Choosing a breeder is an important first step in dog ownership. Fortunately, a majority of Australian Terrier breeders are devoted to the breed and its well-being. Potential owners should be able to find a reputable breeder who lives in their state or region. If you have to travel some distance to reach a good breeder, remember that it's worth the trip!

The American Kennel Club and the breed's parent club, the Australian Terrier Club of America, can refer you to breeders of

PEDIGREE VS. REGISTRATION CERTIFICATE

Too often new owners are confused between these two important documents. Your puppy's pedigree, essentially a family tree, is a written record of a dog's genealogy of three generations or more. The pedigree will show you the names as well as performance titles of all dogs in your pup's background. Your breeder must provide you with a registration application, with his part properly filled out. You must complete the application and send it to the AKC with the proper fee. Every puppy must come from a litter that has been AKC-registered by the breeder, born in the US and from a sire and dam that are also registered with the AKC.

The seller must provide you with complete records to identify the puppy. The AKC requires that the seller provide the buyer with the following: breed; sex, color and markings; date of birth; litter number (when available); names and registration numbers of the parents; breeder's name; and date sold or delivered.

quality Aussies in any part of the country. Potential owners are encouraged to attend dog shows (or other competitive events) to see the Aussies in action, to meet the owners and handlers firsthand and to get an idea of what Australian Terriers look like outside a photographer's lens. Provided you approach the handlers when they are not busy with the dogs, most are more than willing to answer questions, recommend breeders and give advice.

Once you have contacted and met a breeder or two and made your choice about which breeder is best suited to your needs, it's time to visit the litter. Keep in mind that many top breeders have waiting lists. Sometimes new owners have to wait over a year for a puppy. If you are really committed to the breeder whom you've selected, then you will wait (and hope for an early arrival!). If not, you may have to go with your second- or third-choice breeder. Don't be too anxious, however. If the breeder doesn't have a waiting list, or any customers, there is probably a good reason.

Since you are likely to be choosing an Australian Terrier as a pet dog and not a show dog, you simply should select a pup that is healthy, friendly and attractive. Australian Terriers have relatively small litters, averaging four or five puppies, so selection is somewhat limited once you have located a desirable litter. Your selection of a male or female pup is purely personal preference, but males tend to be slightly more aggressive than females.

Breeders commonly allow visitors to see the litters by around the fifth or sixth week, and puppies leave for their new homes between the eighth and tenth week. Breeders who permit their puppies to leave early are more interested in your money than in their puppies' well-being. Puppies need to learn the rules of the pack from their dams, and most dams continue teaching the pups manners and dos and don'ts until at least the eighth week. Breeders spend significant amounts of time with the Aussie toddlers so that they are able to interact with the "other species" i.e., humans. Given the long history that dogs and humans have, bonding between the two species is natural but must be nurtured. A well-bred, well-socialized Australian Terrier pup wants nothing more than to be near you and please you.

SIGNS OF A HEALTHY PUPPY

Healthy puppies are robust little fellows who are alert and active, sporting shiny coats and supple skin. They should not appear lethargic, bloated or pot-bellied, nor should they have flaky skin or runny or crusted eyes or noses. Their stools should be firm and well formed, with no evidence of blood or mucus.

Always check the bite of your selected puppy to be sure that it is neither overshot nor undershot. This may not be too noticeable on a young puppy but will become more noticeable as the puppy matures.

The time spent with his dam and littermates is invaluable to a developing puppy. Many life lessons are learned before the pup leaves his canine pack to become part of a human family.

A COMMITTED NEW OWNER

By now you should understand what makes the Australian Terrier a most unique and special dog, one that may fit nicely into your family and lifestyle. If you have researched breeders, you should be able to recognize a knowledgeable and responsible Australian Terrier breeder who cares not only about his pups but also about what kind of owner you will be. If you have completed the final step in your new journey, you have found a litter, or possibly two, of quality Australian Terrier pups.

A visit with the puppies and their breeder should be an education in itself. Breed research, breeder selection and

NEW RELEASES

Most breeders release their puppies between eight to ten weeks of age. A breeder who allows puppies to leave the litter at five or six weeks of age may be more concerned with profit than with the puppies' welfare. However, some breeders of show or working breeds may hold one or more top-quality puppies longer, occasionally until three or four months of age, in order to evaluate the puppies' career or show potential and decide which one(s) they will keep for themselves.

puppy visitation are very important aspects of finding the puppy of your dreams. Beyond that, these things also lay the foundation for a successful future with your pup. Puppy personalities within each litter vary, from the shy and easygoing puppy to the one who is dominant and assertive, with most pups falling somewhere in between. By spending time with the puppies you will be able to recognize certain behaviors and what these behaviors indicate about each pup's temperament. Which type of pup will complement your family dynamics is best determined by observing the puppies in action within their "pack." Your breeder's expertise and recommendations are also valuable. Although you may fall in love with a bold and brassy male, the breeder may suggest that another pup would be best for you. The breeder's experience in rearing Australian Terrier pups and matching their temperaments with appropriate humans offers the best assurance that your pup will meet your needs and expectations. The type of puppy that you select is just as important as your decision that the Australian Terrier is the breed for you.

The decision to live with an Australian Terrier is a serious commitment and not one to be taken lightly. This puppy is a living sentient being that will be dependent on you for basic survival for his entire life. Beyond the basics of survival—food, water, shelter and protection—he needs much, much more. The new pup needs love, nurturing and a proper canine education to mold him into a responsible, well-behaved canine citizen. Your Australian Terrier's health and good manners will need consistent monitoring and regular "tune-ups," so your job as a responsible dog owner will be ongoing throughout every stage of his life. If you are not prepared to accept these responsibilities and commit to them for the next decade, likely longer, then you are not prepared to own a dog of any breed.

Although the responsibilities of owning a dog may at times tax your patience, the joy of living with your Aussie far outweighs the workload, and a well-mannered adult dog is worth your time and effort. Before your very eyes, your new charge will grow up to be your most loyal friend, devoted to you unconditionally.

YOUR AUSTRALIAN TERRIER SHOPPING LIST

Just as expectant parents prepare a nursery for their baby, so should you ready your home for the arrival of your Australian Terrier pup. If you have the necessary puppy supplies purchased and in place before he comes home, it will ease the puppy's transition from the warmth and familiarity of his mom and littermates to the brand-new environment of his new home and human family. You will be too busy to stock up and prepare your house after your pup comes home, that's for sure! Imagine how a pup must feel upon being transported to a strange new place. It's up to you to comfort him and to let your little pup know that he is going to be happy with you.

Along with a terrier puppy come those notorious terrier puppy teeth! All terriers, regardless of size, have strong teeth and jaws.

MOTHERLY MOODINESS

When selecting a puppy, be certain to meet the dam of the litter. The temperament of the dam is often predictive of the temperament of her puppies. However, dams occasionally are very protective of their young, some to the point of being testy or aggressive with visitors, whom they may view as a danger to their babies. Such attitudes are more common when the pups are very young and still nursing and should not be mistaken for actual aggressive temperament. If possible, visit the dam away from her pups to make friends with her and gain a better understanding of her true personality.

FOOD AND WATER BOWLS

Your puppy will need separate bowls for his food and water. Stainless steel pans are generally preferred over plastic bowls since they sterilize better and pups are less inclined to chew on the metal. Heavy-duty ceramic bowls are popular, but consider how often you will have to pick up those heavy bowls. Buy adult-sized pans, as your Aussie puppy will grow into them before you know it, although he will never need very large bowls.

The Dog Crate

If you think that crates are tools of punishment and confinement for when a dog has misbehaved, think again. Most breeders and almost all trainers recommend a crate as the preferred house-training aid as well as for all-around puppy training and safety. Because dogs are natural den creatures that prefer cave-like environments, the benefits of crate use are many. The crate provides the puppy with his very own "safe house," a cozy place to sleep, take a break or seek comfort with a favorite toy; a travel aid to house your dog when on the road, at motels or at the vet's office; a training aid to help teach your puppy proper toileting habits; a place of solitude when non-dog people happen to drop by and don't want a lively puppy—or even a well-behaved adult dog—saying hello or begging for their attention.

GETTING ACQUAINTED

When visiting a litter, ask the breeder for suggestions on how best to interact with the puppies. If possible, get right into the middle of the pack and sit down with them. Observe which pups climb into your lap and which ones shy away. Toss a toy for them to chase and bring back to you. It's easy to fall in love with the puppy who picks you, but keep your future objectives in mind before you make your final decision.

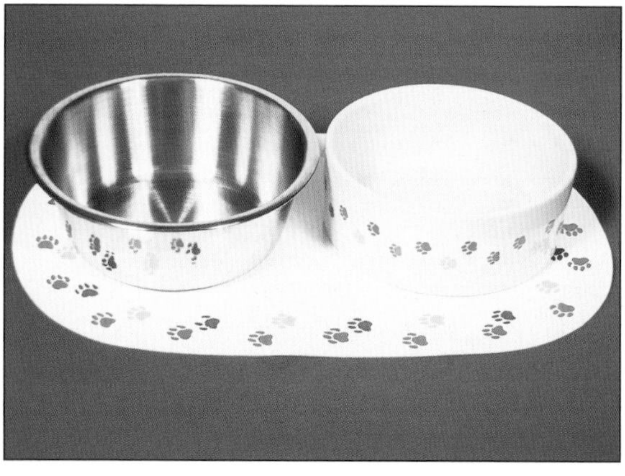

Purchase sturdy, easy-to-clean, chew-resistant bowls for your Aussie.

Crates come in several types, although the wire crate and the fiberglass airline-type crate are the most popular. Both are safe and your puppy will adjust to either one, so the choice is up to you. The wire crates offer better visibility for the pup as well as better ventilation. Many of the wire crates easily fold down, making them easy to carry. The fiberglass crates, similar to those used by the airlines for animal transport,

Your Australian Terrier can use the same crate throughout his life, provided that you purchase and acclimate your pup to a crate that will be large enough for him when fully grown.

Your local pet shop should have a selection of crates from which you can choose the type that best suits your needs.

are sturdier and more den-like. However, the fiberglass crates do not collapse and are less ventilated than wire crates, which can be problematic in hot weather. Some of the newer crates are made of heavy plastic mesh; they are very lightweight and fold up into slim-line suitcases. However, a mesh crate might not be suitable for a pup with manic chewing habits.

Don't bother with a puppy-sized crate. Although your Australian Terrier will be a wee fellow when you bring him home, he will grow up in the blink of an eye and your tiny puppy crate will be useless. Purchase a crate that will accommodate an adult Australian Terrier. He will stand about 10–11 inches at the shoulder when full grown, so a small crate, about 24 inches long by 20 inches wide by 21 inches high, will fit him nicely.

Bedding and Crate Pads

Your puppy will enjoy some type of soft bedding in his "room" (the crate), something he can snuggle into to feel cozy and secure. Old towels or blankets are good choices for a young pup, since he may (and probably will) have a toileting accident or two in the crate or decide to chew on the bedding material. Once he is fully trained and out of the early chewing stage, you can replace the puppy bedding with a permanent crate pad if you prefer. Crate pads and other dog beds run the gamut from inexpensive to high-end doggie-designer styles, but don't splurge on the good stuff until you are sure that your puppy is reliable and won't tear it up or make a mess on it.

Puppy Toys

Just as infants and older children require objects to stimulate their minds and bodies, puppies need toys to entertain their curious brains, wiggly paws and achy teeth. A fun array of safe doggie toys will help satisfy your puppy's chewing instincts and distract him from gnawing on the leg of your antique chair or your new leather sofa. Most puppy toys are cute and look as if they would be a lot of fun, but not all are necessarily safe or good for your puppy, so use caution when you go puppy-toy shopping.

Australian Terriers love to chew! Train your Aussie to chew only on appropriate toys as a pup, because all terriers will chew if bored, and they have strong teeth and jaws. The best "chewcifiers" are sturdy nylon and hard rubber bones, which are safe to gnaw on and come in sizes appropriate for all age groups and breeds. Be especially careful of natural bones, which can splinter or develop dangerous sharp edges; pups can easily swallow or choke on those bone splinters. Veterinarians often tell of surgical nightmares involving bits of splintered bone, because in addition to the danger of choking, the sharp pieces can damage the intestinal tract.

Those who own the breed thoroughly enjoy the company of their charming Aussies.

Similarly, rawhide chews, while a favorite of most dogs and puppies, can be equally dangerous. Pieces of rawhide are easily swallowed after they get all gummy from chewing, and dogs have been known to choke on large pieces of ingested rawhide. Rawhide chews should be offered only when you can supervise the puppy.

Soft woolly toys are special puppy favorites. They come in a

CRATE EXPECTATIONS

To make the crate more inviting to your puppy, you can offer his first meal or two inside the crate, always keeping the crate door open so that he does not feel confined. Keep a favorite toy or two in the crate for him to play with while inside. You can also cover the crate at night with a lightweight sheet to make it more den-like and remove the stimuli of household activity. Never put him into his crate as punishment or as you are scolding him, since he will then associate his crate with negative situations and avoid going there.

Puppy curiosity cannot be curbed! Breeders certainly have their hands full when raising exuberant Aussie litters.

wide variety of cute shapes and sizes; some look like little stuffed animals. Puppies love to shake them up and toss them about, or simply carry them around. However, soft toys are no match for terrier teeth! Be careful of fuzzy toys that have button eyes or noses that your pup could chew off and swallow, and make sure that he does not disembowel a squeaky toy to remove the squeaker! Braided rope toys are similar in that they are fun to chew and toss around, but they shred easily and the strings are easy to swallow. The strings are not digestible and, if the puppy doesn't pass them in his stool, he could end up at the vet's office. As with rawhides, your puppy should be closely monitored with rope toys.

If you believe that your pup has ingested a piece of a toy, check his stools for the next couple of days to see if he passes the item when he defecates. At the same time, also watch for signs of intestinal distress. A call to your veterinarian might be in order to get his advice and be on the safe side.

An all-time favorite toy for puppies (young and old!) is the empty gallon milk jug. Hard plastic juice containers—46 ounces or more—are also excellent. Such containers make lots of noise when they are batted about, and puppies go crazy with delight as they play with them. However, they don't last very long, so be

TEETHING TIME

All puppies chew. It's normal canine behavior. Chewing just plain feels good to a puppy, especially during the three- to five-month teething period when the adult teeth are breaking through the gums. Rather than attempting to eliminate such a strong natural chewing instinct, you will be more successful if you redirect it and teach your puppy what he may or may not chew. Correct inappropriate chewing with a sharp "No!" and offer him a chew toy, praising him when he takes it. Don't become discouraged. Chewing usually decreases after the adult teeth have come in.

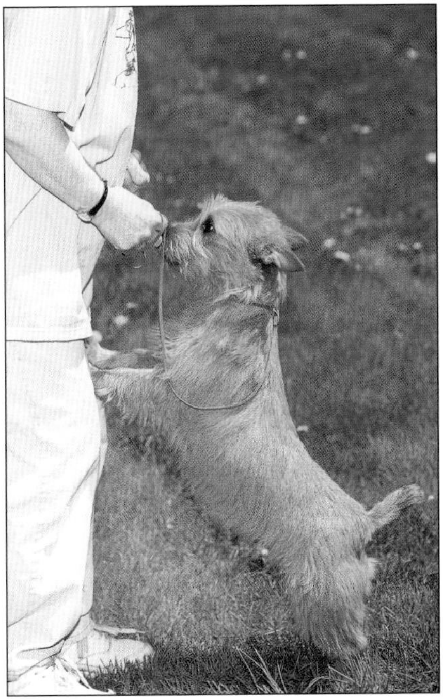

sure to remove and replace them when they get chewed up.

A word of caution about homemade toys: be careful with your choices of non-traditional play objects. Never use old shoes or socks, since a puppy cannot distinguish between the old ones on which he's allowed to chew and the new ones in your closet that are strictly off limits. That principle applies to anything that resembles something that you don't want your puppy to chew.

Collars

A lightweight nylon collar is the best choice for a very young pup. Quick-clip collars are easy to put

TOYS 'R SAFE

The vast array of tantalizing puppy is staggering. Stroll through any pet shop or pet-supply outlet and you will see that the choices can be overwhelming. However, not all dog toys are safe or sensible. Most very young puppies enjoy soft woolly toys that they can snuggle with and carry around. (You know they have outgrown them when they shred them up!) Avoid toys that have buttons, tabs or other enhancements that can be chewed off and swallowed. Soft toys that squeak are fun, but make sure your puppy does not disembowel the toy and remove (and swallow) the squeaker. Toys that rattle or make noise can excite a puppy, but they present the same danger as the squeaky kind and so require supervision. Hard rubber toys that bounce can also entertain a pup, but make sure that the toy is too big for your pup to swallow.

Nothing encourages good behavior like a tasty reward! Be sure to pick up healthy dog treats when shopping for your new family member.

Collaring Our Canines

The standard flat collar with a buckle or a snap, in leather, nylon or cotton, is widely regarded as the everyday all-purpose collar. If the collar fits correctly, you should be able to fit two fingers between the collar and the dog's neck.

The martingale, Greyhound or limited-slip collar is preferred by many dog owners and trainers. It is fixed with an extra loop that tightens when pressure is applied to the leash. The martingale collar gets tighter but does not "choke" the dog. The limited-slip collar should only be used for walking and training, not for free play or interaction with another dog. These types of collar should never be left on the dog, as the extra loop can lead to accidents.

Leather Buckle Collars

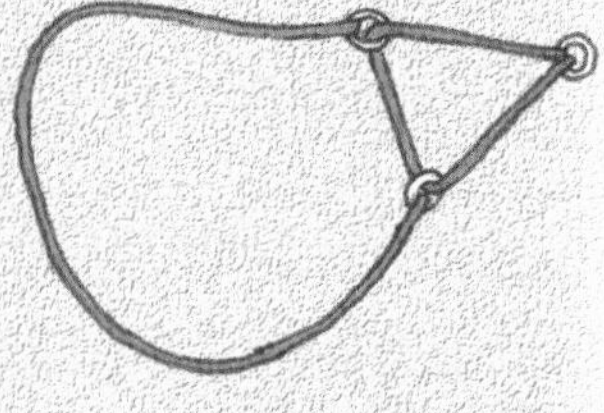

Limited-Slip Collar

Choke collars, usually made of stainless steel, are made for training purposes, though are not recommended for small dogs or heavily coated breeds. The chains can injure small dogs or damage long/abundant coats. Thin nylon choke leads are commonly used on show dogs while in the ring, though they are not practical for everyday use.

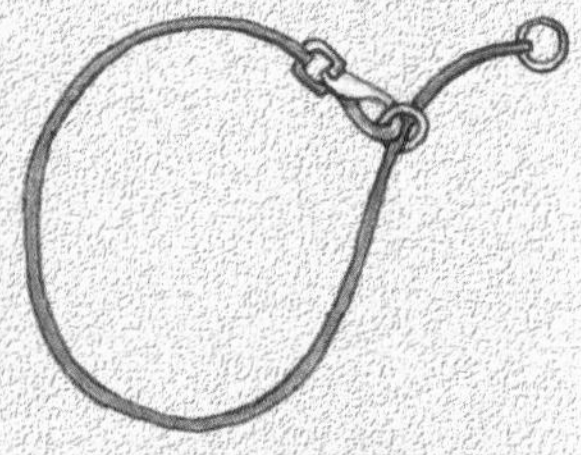

Snap Bolt Choke Collar

The harness, with two or three straps that attach over the dog's shoulders and around his torso, is a humane and safe alternative to the conventional collar. By and large, a well-made harness is virtually escape-proof. Harnesses are available in nylon and mesh and can be outfitted on most dogs, with chest girths ranging from 10 to 30 inches.

Harness

Nylon Collar

Quick-Click Closure

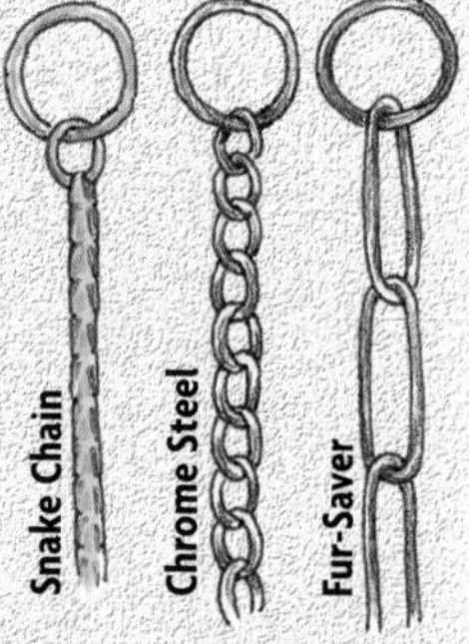

Choke Chain Collars

A head collar, composed of a nylon strap that goes around the dog's muzzle and a second strap that wraps around his neck, offers the owner better control over his dog. This device is recommended for problem-solving with dogs (including jumping up, pulling and aggressive behaviors), but must be used with care.

A training halter, including a flat collar and two straps, made of nylon and webbing, is designed for walking. There are several on the market; some are more difficult to put on the dog than others. The halter harness, with two small slip rings at each end, is recommended for ease of use.

on and remove, and they can be adjusted as the puppy grows. Introduce him to his collar as soon as he comes home to get him accustomed to wearing it. He'll get used to it quickly and won't mind a bit. Make sure that it is snug enough that it won't slip off, yet loose enough to be comfortable for the pup. You should be able to slip two fingers between the collar and his neck. Check the collar often, as puppies grow in spurts, and his collar can become too tight almost overnight. Choke collars are for training purposes only, but should never be used on an Australian Terrier. Explore other training collar options, such as the head collar.

Leashes

A 6-foot nylon lead is an excellent choice for a young puppy. It is lightweight and not as tempting to chew as a leather lead. You can switch to a 6-foot leather lead after your pup has grown and is used to walking politely on a lead. For initial puppy walks and house-training purposes, you should invest in a shorter lead so that you have more control over the puppy. At first, you don't want him wandering too far away from you, and when taking him out for toileting you will want to keep him in the specific area chosen for his potty spot.

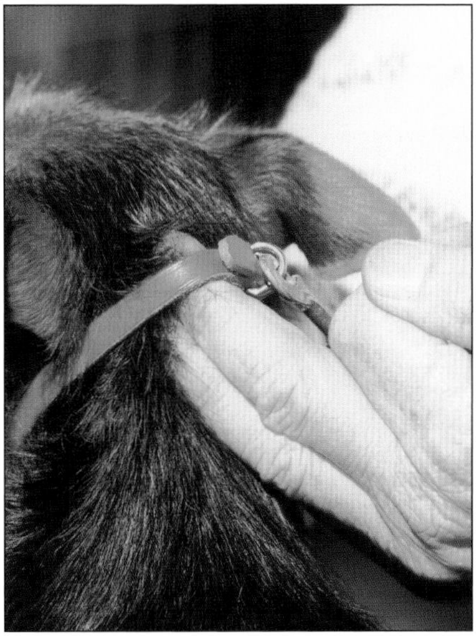

A lightweight adjustable collar, leather or nylon, is suitable for your Aussie puppy.

Once the puppy is heel-trained with a traditional leash, you can consider purchasing a retractable lead. This type of lead is excellent for walking adult dogs that are already leash-wise. The retractable allows the dog to roam farther away from you and explore a wider area when out walking (much appreciated by a curious terrier!), and also retracts when you need to keep him close to you.

HOME SAFETY FOR YOUR PUPPY

The importance of puppy-proofing cannot be overstated. In addition to making your house comfortable for your Australian Terrier's arrival, you also must make sure that your house is safe for your puppy before you bring him home.

Leash Life

Dogs love leashes! Believe it or not, most dogs dance for joy every time their owners pick up their leashes. The leash means that the dog is going for a walk—and there are few things more exciting than that! Here are some of the kinds of leashes that are commercially available.

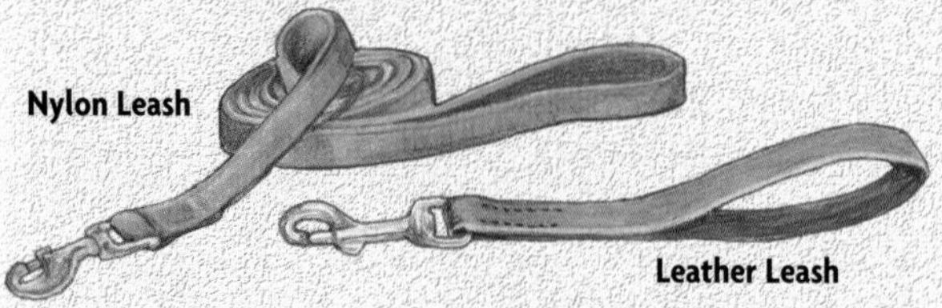

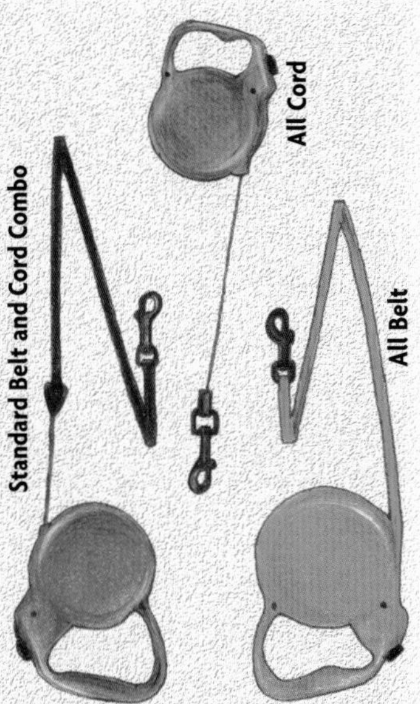

Retractable Leashes

Traditional Leash: Made of cotton, nylon or leather, these leashes are usually about 6 feet in length. A quality-made leather leash is softer on the hands than a nylon one. Durable woven cotton is a popular option. Lengths can vary up to about 48 feet, designed for different uses.

Chain Leash: Usually a metal chain leash with a plastic handle. This is not the best choice for most breeds, as it is heavier than other leashes and difficult to manage.

Retractable Leash: A long nylon cord is housed in a plastic device for extending and retracting. This leash is ideal for taking trained dogs for long walks in open areas, although it is not recommended for large, powerful breeds. Different lengths and sizes are available, so check that you purchase one appropriate for your dog's weight.

Elastic Leash: A nylon leash with an elastic extension. This is useful for well-trained dogs, especially in conjunction with a head halter. Avoid leashes that are completely elastic, as they afford minimal control to the handler.

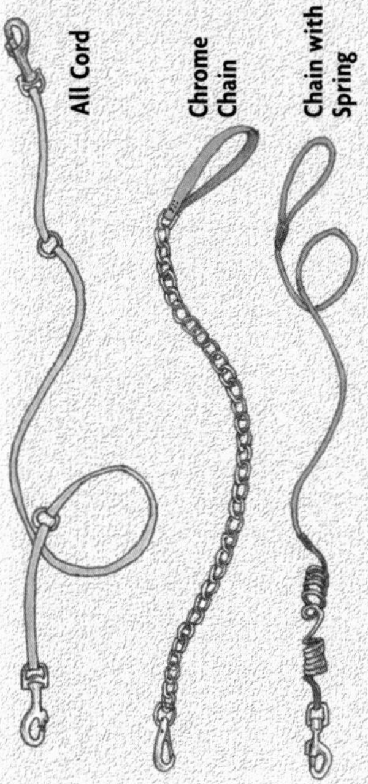

Adjustable Leash: This has two snaps, one on each end, and several metal rings. It is handy if you need to tether your dog temporarily, but is never to be used with a choke collar.

Tab Leash: A short leash (4 to 6 inches long) that attaches to your dog's collar. This device serves like a handle, in case you have to grab your dog while he's exercising off lead. It's ideal for "half-trained" dogs or dogs that listen only half the time.

Slip Leash: Essentially a leash with a collar built in, similar to what a dog-show handler uses to show a dog. This British-style collar has a ring on the end so that you can form a slip collar. Useful if you have to catch your own runaway dog or a stray.

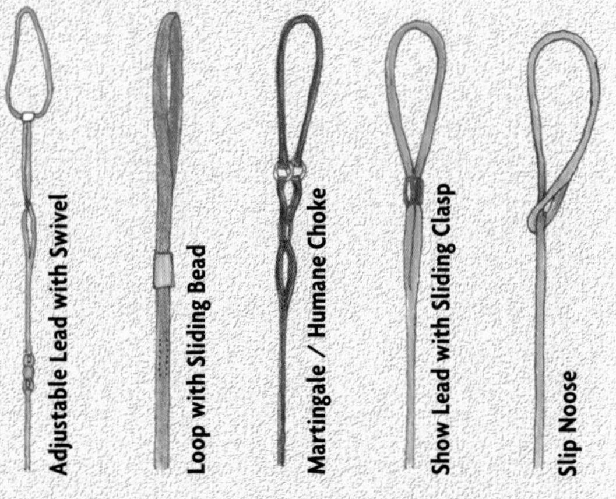

A Variety of Collar-and-Leash-in-One Products

There are countless hazards in the owner's personal living environment that a pup can sniff, chew, swallow or destroy. Many are obvious; others are not. Do a thorough advance house check to remove or rearrange those things that could hurt your puppy, keeping any potentially dangerous items out of areas to which he will have access.

Electrical cords are especially dangerous, since puppies view them as irresistible chew toys. Unplug and remove all exposed cords or fasten them beneath the baseboards where the puppy cannot reach them. Veterinarians and firefighters can tell you horror stories about electrical burns and house fires that resulted from puppy-chewed electrical cords. Consider this a most serious precaution for your puppy and the rest of your family.

All dogs, pups and adults alike, need clean fresh water for good health. This young Aussie would rather take a bath than a drink!

Scout your home for tiny objects that might be seen at a pup's eye level. Keep medication bottles and cleaning supplies well out of reach, and do the same with waste baskets and other trash containers. It goes without saying that you should not use rodent poison or other toxic chemicals in any puppy area and that you must keep such containers safely locked up. You will be amazed at how many places a curious puppy can discover!

Once your house has cleared inspection, check your yard. A sturdy fence will give your dog a safe place to play and potty. Although Australian Terriers are

SWEETS THAT KILL

Antifreeze would be every dog's favorite topping for a chocolate sundae! However, antifreeze, just like chocolate, kills dogs. Ethylene glycol, found in antifreeze, causes acute renal failure in dogs and can be fatal. Dogs suffering from kidney failure expel little or no urine, act lethargically, may experience vomiting or diarrhea and may resist activity and drinking water. Just a single teaspoon of antifreeze is enough to kill a dog (depending on the size); even for large dogs it takes only a tablespoon or two! Like that irresistible chocolate, antifreeze is sweet-tasting and smells yummy. Keep both away from your dog!

not known to be climbers or fence jumpers, they are still athletic dogs, so a 5-foot-high fence should be adequate to contain an agile youngster or adult. It is also essential that the fence is well-embedded into the ground (about a foot deep). All terriers are talented diggers and an Aussie can easily dig a hole big enough for him to squeeze under a fence. Check the fence periodically for necessary repairs. If there is a weak link or space to squeeze through, you can be sure a determined Australian Terrier will discover it.

The garage and shed can be hazardous places for a pup, as things like fertilizers, chemicals and tools are usually kept there. It's best to keep these areas off limits to the pup. Antifreeze is especially dangerous to dogs, as they find the taste appealing and it takes only a few licks from the driveway to kill a dog, puppy or adult, small breed or large.

TOXIC PLANTS

Plants are natural puppy magnets, but many can be harmful, even fatal, if ingested by a puppy or adult dog. Scout your yard and home interior and remove any plants, bushes or flowers that could be even mildly dangerous. It could save your puppy's life. You can obtain a complete list of toxic plants from your veterinarian, at the public library or by looking online.

VISITING THE VETERINARIAN

A good veterinarian is your Australian Terrier puppy's best health-insurance policy. If you do not already have a vet, ask friends and experienced dog people in your area for recommendations so that you can select a vet before you bring your Australian Terrier puppy home. Also arrange for your puppy's first veterinary examination beforehand, since many vets have two- and three-week waiting periods and your puppy should visit the vet within a day or so of coming home.

It's important to make sure your puppy's first visit to the vet is a pleasant and positive one. The vet should take great care to befriend the pup and handle him gently to make their first meeting a positive experience. The vet will give the pup a thorough physical examination and set up a schedule for vaccinations and other necessary wellness visits. Be sure to show your vet any health and

THE GRASS IS ALWAYS GREENER

Must dog owners decide between their beloved canine pals and their perfectly manicured emerald-green lawns? Just as dog urine is no tonic for growing grass, lawn chemicals are extremely dangerous to your dog. Fertilizers, pesticides and herbicides pose real threats to canines and humans alike. Dogs should be kept off treated grounds for at least 24 hours following treatment. Consider some organic options for your lawn care, such as using a homemade compost or a natural fertilizer instead of a commercial chemical. Some dog-conscious lawnkeepers avoid fertilizers entirely, keeping up their lawns by watering, aerating, mowing and seeding frequently.

As always, dogs complicate the equation. Canines love grass. They roll in it, eat it and love to bury their noses in it—and then do their business in it! Grass can mean hours of feel-good, smell-good fun! In addition to the dangers of lawn-care chemicals, there's also the threat of burs, thorns and pebbles in the grass, not to mention the very common grass allergy. Many dogs develop an incurably itchy skin condition from grass, especially in the late summer when the world is in full bloom.

Home safety for your Aussie pup means indoors and out.

inoculation records, which you should have received from your breeder. Your vet is a great source of canine health information, so be sure to ask questions and take notes. Creating a health journal for your puppy will make a handy reference for his wellness and any future health problems that may arise.

MEETING THE FAMILY

Your Australian Terrier's homecoming is an exciting time for all members of the family, and it's only natural that everyone will be eager to meet him, pet him and play with him. However, for the puppy's sake, it's best to make these initial family meetings as uneventful as possible so that the pup is not overwhelmed with too much too soon. Remember, he has just left his dam and his littermates and is away from the breeder's home for the first time. Despite his fuzzy wagging tail, he is still apprehensive and wondering where he is and who all these

Don't let your snooping Aussie follow his nose into danger.

strange humans are. It's best to let him explore on his own and meet the family members as he feels comfortable. Let him investigate all the new smells, sights and sounds at his own pace. Children should be especially careful to not get overly excited, use loud voices or hug the pup too tightly. Be calm, gentle and affectionate, and be ready to comfort him if he appears frightened or uneasy.

Be sure to show your puppy his new crate during this first day home. Toss a treat or two inside the crate; if he associates the crate with food, he will associate the crate with good things. If he is comfortable with the crate, you can offer him his first meal inside it. Leave the door ajar so he can wander in and out as he chooses.

FIRST NIGHT IN HIS NEW HOME

So much has happened in your Australian Terrier puppy's first day away from the breeder. He's had his first car ride to his new home. He's met his new human family and perhaps the other family pets. He has explored his new house and yard, at least those places where he is to be allowed during his first weeks at home. He may have visited his new veterinarian. He has eaten his first meal or two away from his dam and littermates. Surely that's enough to tire out an eight-week-old Australian Terrier pup…or so you hope!

It's bedtime. During the day, the pup investigated his crate, which is his new den and sleep-

DIGGING OUT

Some dogs love to dig. Others wouldn't think of it. With an Aussie, you're dealing with an "earth dog." Digging is considered "self-rewarding behavior" because it's fun! Of all the digging solutions offered by the experts, most are only marginally successful and none is guaranteed to work. The best cure is prevention, which means removing the dog from the offending site when he digs as well as distracting him when you catch him digging so that he turns his attentions elsewhere. That means that you have to supervise your dog's yard time. An unsupervised digger can create havoc with your landscaping or, worse, run away!

ing space, so it is not entirely strange to him. Line the crate with a soft towel or blanket that he can snuggle into and gently place him into the crate for the night. Some breeders send home a piece of bedding from where the pup slept with his littermates, and those familiar scents are a great comfort for the puppy on his first night without his siblings.

He will probably whine or cry. The puppy is objecting to the confinement and the fact that he is alone for the first time. This can be a stressful time for you as well as for the pup. It's important that you remain strong and don't let the puppy out of his crate to comfort him. He will fall asleep eventually. If you release him, the puppy will learn that crying means "out" and will continue that habit. You are laying the groundwork for future habits. Some breeders find that soft music can soothe a crying pup and help him get to sleep.

FIRST CAR RIDE

The ride to your home from the breeder will no doubt be your puppy's first automobile experience, and you should make every effort to keep him comfortable and secure. Bring a large towel or small blanket for the puppy to lie on during the trip and an extra towel in case the pup gets carsick or has a potty accident. It's best to have another person with you to hold the puppy in his lap. Most puppies will fall fast asleep from the rolling motion of the car. If the ride is lengthy, you may have to stop so that the puppy can relieve himself, so be sure to bring a leash and collar for those stops. Avoid rest areas for potty trips, since those are frequented by many dogs, who may carry parasites or disease. It's better to stop at grassy areas near gas stations or shopping centers to prevent unhealthy exposure for your pup.

SOCIALIZING YOUR PUPPY

The next 20 weeks of your Australian Terrier puppy's life are the most important of his entire lifetime. A properly socialized puppy will grow up to be a confident and stable adult who will be a pleasure to live with and a welcome addition to the neighborhood.

The importance of socialization cannot be overemphasized. Research on canine behavior has proven that puppies who are not exposed to new sights, sounds, people and animals during their first 20 weeks of life will grow up to be timid and fearful, even aggressive, and unable to flourish outside of their familiar home environment.

Socializing your puppy is not difficult and, in fact, will be a fun time for you both. Lead training goes hand in hand with socialization, so your puppy will be learning how to walk on a lead at the same time that he's meeting the neighborhood. Because the Australian Terrier is such a terrific breed, your puppy will enjoy being "the new kid on the block." Take him for short walks, to the park and to other dog-friendly places where he will encounter new people, especially children. Puppies automatically recognize children as "little people" and are drawn to play with them. Just make sure that you supervise these meetings and that the children do not get too rough or encourage him to play too hard. An overzealous pup can often nip too hard, frightening the child and in turn making the puppy overly excited. A bad experience in puppyhood can impact a dog for life, so a pup that has a negative experience with a child may grow up to be shy or even aggressive around children.

Take your puppy along on your daily errands. Puppies are natural "people magnets," and most people who see your pup will want to pet him. All of these encounters will help to mold him into a confident adult dog. Likewise, you will soon feel like a confident, responsible dog owner, rightly proud of your handsome Australian Terrier.

Be especially careful of your puppy's encounters and experiences during the eight-to-ten-week-old period, which is also called the "fear period." This is a serious imprinting period, and all contact during this time should be gentle and positive. A frightening or negative event could leave a permanent impression that could affect his future behavior if a similar situation arises.

Also make sure that your puppy has received his first and second rounds of vaccinations before you expose him to other dogs or bring him to places that other dogs may frequent. Avoid dog parks and other strange-dog areas until your vet assures you that your puppy is fully immunized and resistant to the diseases

THE FAMILY FELINE

A resident cat has feline squatter's rights. The cat will treat the newcomer (your puppy) as she sees fit, regardless of what you do or say. So it's best to let the two of them work things out on their own terms. Cats have a height advantage and will generally leap to higher ground to avoid direct contact with a rambunctious pup. Some will hiss and boldly swat at a pup who passes by or tries to reach the cat. Keep the puppy under control in the presence of the cat and they will eventually become accustomed to each other.

Here's a hint: move the cat's litter box where the puppy can't get into it! It's best to do so well before the pup comes home so the cat is used to the new location.

that can be passed between canines. Discuss socialization with your breeder, as some breeders recommend socializing the puppy even before he has received all of his inoculations, depending on how outgoing the puppy may be.

LEADER OF THE PUPPY'S PACK

Like other canines, your puppy needs an authority figure, someone he can look up to and regard as the leader of his "pack." His first pack leader was his dam, who taught him to be polite and not chew too hard on her ears or nip at her muzzle. He learned those same lessons from his littermates. If he played too rough, they cried in pain and stopped the game, which sent an important message to the rowdy puppy.

As puppies play together, they are also struggling to determine who will be the boss. Being pack animals, dogs need someone to be in charge. If a litter of puppies remained together beyond puppyhood, one of the pups would emerge as the strongest one, the one who calls the shots.

Once your puppy leaves the pack, he will look intuitively for a new leader. If he does not recognize you as that leader, he will try to assume that position for himself. Of course, it is hard to imagine your adorable Australian Terrier puppy trying to be in charge when he is so small and seemingly helpless. You must remember that these are natural canine instincts. Do not cave in and allow your pup to get the upper "paw"!

Just as socialization is so important during these first 20 weeks, so too is your puppy's

Well-socialized puppies grow into loving, affectionate adult dogs, as this kissing Aussie happily displays.

PUPPY PARASITES

Parasites are nasty little critters that live in or on your dog or puppy. Most puppies are born with ascarid roundworms, which are acquired from dormant ascarids residing in the dam. Other parasites can be acquired through contact with infected fecal matter. Take a stool sample to your vet for testing. He will prescribe a safe wormer to treat any parasites found in your puppy's stool. Always have a fecal test performed at your puppy's annual veterinary exam.

Socialization is essential to all dogs, but especially to show dogs, as aggression toward other dogs is not tolerated in the ring or on the show grounds.

early education. He was born without any bad habits. He does not know what is good or bad behavior. If he does things like nipping and digging, it's because he is having fun and doesn't know that humans consider these things as "bad." It's your job to teach him proper puppy manners, and this is the best time to accomplish that...before he has developed bad habits, since it is much more difficult to "unlearn" or correct unacceptable learned behavior than to teach good behavior from the start.

Make sure that all members of the family understand the importance of being consistent when training their new puppy. If you tell the puppy to stay off the sofa and your daughter allows him to cuddle on the couch with her to watch her favorite television show, your pup will be confused about what he is and is not allowed to do. Have a family conference before your pup comes home so that everyone understands the basic principles of puppy training and the rules you have set forth for the pup, and agrees to follow them.

PUPPY PROBLEM PREVENTION

The old saying that "an ounce of prevention is worth a pound of cure" is especially true when it comes to puppies. It is much easier to prevent inappropriate behavior than it is to change it. It's also easier and less stressful for the pup, since it will keep discipline to a minimum and create a more positive learning environment for him. That, in turn, will also be easier on you!

Here are a few commonsense tips to keep your belongings safe and your puppy out of trouble:

- Keep your closet doors closed

BE CONSISTENT

Consistency is a key element, in fact is absolutely necessary, to a puppy's learning environment. A behavior (such as chewing, jumping up or climbing onto the furniture) cannot be forbidden one day and then allowed the next. That will only confuse the pup, and he will not understand what he is supposed to do. Just one or two episodes of allowing an undesirable behavior to "slide" will imprint that behavior on a puppy's brain and make that behavior more difficult to erase or change.

and your shoes, socks and other apparel off the floor so your puppy can't get at them.

- Keep a secure lid on the trash container or put the trash where your puppy can't dig into it. He can't damage what he can't reach!
- Supervise your puppy at all times to make sure he is not getting into mischief. If he starts to chew the corner of the rug, you can distract him instantly by tossing a toy for him to fetch. You also will be able to whisk him outside when you notice that he is about to piddle on the carpet. If you can't see your puppy, you can't teach him or correct his behavior.

Chewing and Nipping

Nipping at fingers and toes is normal puppy behavior. Chewing is also the way that puppies investigate their surroundings. However, you will have to teach your puppy that chewing anything other than his toys is not acceptable. That won't happen overnight and at times puppy teeth will test your patience. However, if you allow nipping and chewing to continue, just think about the damage that a mature Australian Terrier can do with a full set of adult terrier teeth.

Whenever your puppy nips your hand or fingers, cry out "Ouch!" in a loud voice, which should startle your puppy and stop him from nipping, even if

> **CONFINEMENT**
>
> It is wise to keep your puppy confined to a small "puppy-proofed" area of the house for his first few weeks at home. Gate or block off a space near the door he will use for outdoor potty trips. Expandable baby gates are useful to create puppy's designated area. If he is allowed to roam through the entire house or even only several rooms, it will be more difficult to house-train him.

As two dogs meet, they sniff and posture as they familiarize themselves with each other.

Your new Australian Terrier puppy requires love, affection and human handling to make him feel secure and welcome in his new surroundings.

only for a moment. Immediately distract him by offering a small treat or an appropriate toy for him to chew instead (which means having chew toys and puppy treats handy or in your pockets at all times). Praise him when he takes the toy and tell him what a good fellow he is. Praise is just as or even more important in puppy training as discipline and correction.

Puppies also tend to nip at children more often than at adults, since they perceive little ones to be more vulnerable and more similar to their littermates. Teach your children appropriate responses to nipping behavior. If they are unable to handle it themselves, you may have to intervene. Puppy nips can be quite painful and a child's frightened reaction will only encourage a puppy to nip harder, which is a natural canine response. As with all other puppy situations, interaction between your Australian Terrier puppy and children should be supervised.

Chewing on objects, not just family members' fingers and ankles, is also normal canine behavior that can be especially tedious (for the owner, not the pup) during the teething period when the puppy's adult teeth are coming in. At this stage, chewing just plain feels good. Furniture legs and cabinet corners are common puppy favorites. Shoes and other personal items also taste pretty good to a pup.

The best solution is, once again, prevention. If you value something, keep it tucked away and out of reach. You can't hide your dining-room table in a closet, but you can try to deflect the chewing by applying a bitter product made just to deter dogs from chewing. Available in a spray or cream, this substance is vile-tasting, although safe for dogs, and most puppies will avoid the forbidden object after one tiny taste. You also can apply the product to your leather leash if the puppy tries to chew on his lead during leash-training sessions.

Keep a ready supply of safe chews handy to offer your Australian Terrier as a distraction when he starts to chew on something that's a "no-no." Remember,

CREATE A SCHEDULE

Puppies thrive on sameness and routine. Offer meals at the same time each day, take him out at regular times for potty trips and do the same for play periods and outdoor activity. Make note of when your puppy naps and when he is most lively and energetic, and try to plan his day around those times. Once he is house-trained and more predictable in his habits, he will be better able to tolerate changes in his schedule.

WATCH THE WATER

To help your puppy sleep through the night without having to relieve himself, remove his water bowl after 7 p.m. Offer him a couple of ice cubes during the evening to quench his thirst. Never leave water in a puppy's crate, as this is inviting puddles of mishaps.

at this tender age he does not yet know what is permitted or forbidden, so you have to be "on call" every minute he's awake and on the prowl.

You may lose a treasure or two during puppy's growing-up period, and the furniture could sustain a nasty nick or two. These can be trying times, so be prepared for those inevitable accidents and comfort yourself in knowing that this too shall pass.

All dogs are pack animals and prefer the company of other animals, whether they are Australian Terriers or humans!

PUPPY WHINING

Puppies often cry and whine, just as infants and little children do. It's their way of telling us that they are lonely or in need of attention. Your puppy will miss his littermates and will feel insecure when he is left alone. You may be out of the house or just in another room, but he will still feel alone. During these times, the puppy's crate should be his personal comfort station, a place all his own where he can feel safe and secure. Once he learns that being alone is okay and not something to be feared, he will settle down without crying or objecting. You might want to leave a radio on while he is crated, as the sound of human voices can be soothing and will give the impression that people are around.

Give your puppy a favorite cuddly toy or chew toy to entertain him whenever he is crated. You will both be happier: the puppy because he is safe in his den and you because he is quiet, safe and not getting into puppy escapades that can wreak havoc in your house or cause him danger.

Australian Terrier puppies, like other puppies, like to chew on soft things while they are teething.

To make sure that your puppy will always view his crate as a safe and cozy place, never, ever, use the crate as punishment. That's the best way to turn the crate into a negative place that the pup will want to avoid. Sure, you can use the crate for your own peace of mind if your puppy is getting into trouble and needs some "time out." Just don't let him know that! Never scold the pup and immediately place him into the crate. Count to ten, give him a couple of hugs and maybe a treat, then scoot him into his crate.

It's also important not to make a big fuss when he is released from the crate. That will make getting out of the crate more appealing than being in the crate, which is just the opposite of what you are trying to achieve.

THE WORRIES OF MANGE

Sometimes called "puppy mange," demodectic mange is passed to the puppy through the mother's milk. The microscopic mites that cause the condition take up residence in the puppy's hair follicles and sebaceous glands. Stress can cause the mites to multiply, causing bare patches on the face, neck and front legs. If neglected, it can lead to secondary bacterial infections, but if diagnosed and treated early, demodectic mange can be localized and controlled. Most pups recover without complications.

PROPER CARE OF YOUR
AUSTRALIAN TERRIER

Adding a Australian Terrier to your household means adding a new family member who will need your care each and every day. When your Australian Terrier pup first comes home, you will start a routine with him so that, as he grows up, your dog will have a daily schedule just as you do. The aspects of your dog's daily care will likewise become regular parts of your day, so you'll both have a new schedule. Dogs learn by consistency and thrive on routine: regular times for meals, exercise, grooming and potty trips are just as important for your dog as they are to you! Your dog's schedule will depend much on your family's daily routine, but remember that you now have a new member of the family who is part of your day every day.

> **FREE FEEDING**
> Many owners opt to feed their dogs the free way. That is, they serve dry kibble in a feeder that is available to the dog all day. Arguably, this is the most convenient method of feeding an adult dog, but it may encourage the dog to become fussy about food or defensive over his bowl. Free feeding is an option only for adult dogs, not puppies.

FEEDING

Feeding your dog the best diet is based on various factors, including age, activity level, overall condition and size of breed. When you visit the breeder, he will share with you his advice about the proper diet for your dog based on his experience with the breed and the foods with which he has had success. Likewise, your vet will be a helpful source of advice throughout the dog's life and will aid you in planning a diet for optimal health.

FEEDING THE PUPPY

Of course, your pup's very first food will be his dam's milk. There may be special situations in which pups fail to nurse, necessitating that the breeder hand-feed them with a formula, but for the most part pups spend the first weeks of life nursing from their dam. The breeder weans the pups by gradually introducing solid foods and decreasing the milk meals. Pups may even start themselves off on the weaning process, albeit inadvertently, if they snatch bites from their mom's food bowl.

By the time the pups are ready for new homes, they are fully weaned and eating a good puppy food. As a new owner, you may be thinking, "Great! The breeder has taken care of the hard part." Not so fast.

A puppy's first year of life is the time when all or most of his growth and development takes place. This is a delicate time, and diet plays a huge role in proper skeletal and muscular formation. Improper diet and exercise habits can lead to damaging problems that will compromise the dog's health and movement for his entire life. That being said, new owners should not worry needlessly. With the myriad types of food formulated specifically for growing pups of different-sized breeds, dog-food manufacturers have taken much of the guesswork out of feeding your puppy well. Since growth-food formulas are designed to provide the nutrition that a growing puppy needs, it is unnecessary and, in fact, can prove harmful to add supplements to the diet. Research has shown that too much of certain vitamin supplements and minerals predispose a dog to skeletal problems. It's by no means a case of "if a little is good, a lot is better." At every stage of your dog's life, too much or too little in the way of nutrients can be harmful, which is why a manufactured complete food is the easiest way to know that your dog is getting what he needs.

Because of a young pup's small body and accordingly small digestive system, his daily portion will be divided up into small meals throughout the day. This can mean starting off with three or more meals a day and

Kibble overboard! An enthusiastic young eater makes sure he gets every last bite.

HOLD THE ONIONS

Sliced, chopped or grated; dehydrated, boiled, fried or raw; pearl, Spanish, white or red: onions can be deadly to your dog. The toxic effects of onions in dogs are cumulative for up to 30 days. A serious form of anemia, called Heinz body anemia, affects the red blood cells of dogs that have eaten onions. For safety (and better breath), dogs should avoid chives and scallions as well.

Puppies receive essential nutrition from their dams and should be fully weaned by eight weeks of age.

decreasing the number of meals as the pup matures. Eventually you can feed only one meal a day, although it is generally thought that dividing the day's food into two meals on a morning/evening schedule is healthier for the dog's digestion.

Regarding the feeding schedule, feeding the pup at the same times and in the same place each day is important for both housebreaking purposes and establishing the dog's everyday routine. As for the amount to feed, growing puppies generally need proportionately more food per body weight than their adult counterparts, but a pup should never be allowed to gain excess weight. Dogs of all ages should be kept in proper body condition, but extra weight can strain a pup's developing frame, causing skeletal problems.

Watch your pup's weight as he grows and, if the recommended amounts seem to be too much or too little for your pup, consult the vet about appropriate dietary changes. Keep in mind that treats, although small, can quickly add up throughout the day, contributing unnecessary calories. Treats are fine when used prudently; opt for dog treats specially formulated to be healthy or for nutritious snacks like small pieces of cheese or cooked chicken.

Feeding the Adult Dog

For the adult (meaning physically mature) dog, feeding properly is about maintenance, not growth. Again, correct weight is a concern. Your dog should appear fit and should have an evident "waist." His ribs should not be protruding (a sign of being underweight), but they should be covered by only a slight layer of fat. Under normal circumstances, an adult dog can be maintained fairly easily with a high-quality nutritionally complete adult-formula food.

Factor treats into your dog's overall daily caloric intake, and avoid offering table scraps. Overweight dogs are more prone to health problems. Research has even shown that obesity takes years off a dog's life. With that in mind, resist the urge to overfeed and over-treat. Don't make unnecessary additions to your dog's diet, whether with tidbits or with extra vitamins and minerals.

Once you've found a good-quality, balanced, complete dog food, your Aussie can stick with the same food throughout his adult years.

NOT HUNGRY?

No dog in his right mind would turn down his dinner, would he? If you notice that your dog has lost interest in his food, there could be any number of causes. Dental problems are a common cause of appetite loss, one that is often overlooked. If your dog has a toothache, a loose tooth or sore gums from infection, chances are it doesn't feel so good to chew. Think about when you've had a toothache! If your dog does not approach the food bowl with his usual enthusiasm, look inside his mouth for signs of a problem. Whatever the cause, you'll want to consult your vet so that your chow hound can get back to his happy, hungry self as soon as possible.

As hard as it may be, don't give in to your Aussie's pleas! "People food" can cause illness and obesity, not to mention that giving tidbits from your plate encourages begging.

The amount of food needed for proper maintenance will vary depending on the individual dog's activity level, but you will be able to tell whether the daily portions are keeping him in good shape. With the wide variety of good complete foods available, choosing what to feed is largely a matter of personal preference. Just as with the puppy, the adult dog should have consistency in his mealtimes and feeding place. In addition to a consistent routine, regular mealtimes also allow the owner to see how much his dog is eating. If the dog seems never to be satisfied or, likewise, becomes uninterested in his food, the owner will know right away that something is wrong and can consult the vet.

Diets for the Aging Dog

A good rule of thumb is that once a dog has reached 75% of his expected lifespan, he has reached "senior citizen" or geriatric status. Your Australian Terrier will be considered a senior at about 9 years of age; based on his size and breed-specific factors, he has a projected lifespan of about 12–14 years. (The smallest breeds generally enjoy the longest lives and the largest breeds the shortest.)

What does aging have to do with your dog's diet? No, he won't get a discount at the local diner's early-bird special. Yes, he will require some dietary changes to accommodate the changes that come along with increased age. One change is that the older dog's dietary needs become more similar to that of a puppy. Specifically, dogs can metabolize more protein

SAY NUTS TO GRAPES

Small amounts of fresh grapes and raisins can cause vomiting and diarrhea in dogs, possibly even kidney failure in the worst cases. Nuts, in general, are not recommended for dogs. Macadamia nuts, for example, can cause vomiting, diarrhea, fatigue and temporary paralysis of rear legs. Dogs usually recover from these symptoms in a few days. Almonds are also especially problematic for dogs.

as youngsters and seniors than in the adult-maintenance stage. Discuss with your vet whether you need to switch to a higher-protein or senior-formulated food or whether your current adult-dog food contains sufficient nutrition for the senior.

Watching the dog's weight remains essential, even more so in the senior stage. Older dogs are already more vulnerable to illness, and obesity only contributes to their susceptibility to problems. As the older dog becomes less active and thus exercises less, his regular portions may cause him to gain weight. At this point, you may consider decreasing his daily food intake or switching to a reduced-calorie food. As with other changes, you should consult your vet for advice.

Puppies and adults alike need water available to them at all times. Multiple water bowls, kept indoors and outdoors, will keep a thirsty dog satisfied.

DIET DON'TS

- Got milk? Don't give it to your dog! Dogs cannot tolerate large quantities of cows' milk, as they do not have the enzymes to digest lactose.
- You may have heard of dog owners who add raw eggs to their dogs' food for a shiny coat or to make the food more palatable, but consumption of raw eggs too often can cause a deficiency of the vitamin biotin.
- Avoid feeding table scraps, as they will upset the balance of the dog's complete food. Additionally, fatty or highly seasoned foods can cause upset canine stomachs.
- Do not offer raw meat to your dog. Raw meat can contain parasites; it also is high in fat.
- Vitamin A toxicity in dogs can be caused by too much raw liver, especially if the dog already gets enough vitamin A in his balanced diet, which should be the case.
- Bones like chicken, pork chop and other soft bones are not suitable, as they easily splinter.

Types of Food and Reading the Labels

When selecting the type of food to feed your dog, it is important to check out the label for ingredients. Many dry-food products have soybean, corn or rice as the main ingredient. The main ingredient will be listed first on the label, with the rest of the ingredients following in descending order according to their propor-

QUENCHING HIS THIRST

Is your dog drinking more than normal and trying to lap up everything in sight? Excessive drinking has many different causes. Obvious causes for a dog's being thirstier than usual are hot weather and vigorous exercise. However, if your dog is drinking more for no apparent reason, you could have cause for concern. Serious conditions like kidney or liver disease, diabetes and various types of hormonal problems can all be indicated by excessive drinking. If you notice your dog's being excessively thirsty, contact your vet at once. Hopefully there will be a simpler explanation, but the earlier a serious problem is detected, the sooner it can be treated, with a better rate of cure.

tion in the food. While these types of dry food are fine, you should look into dry foods based on meat or fish. These are better-quality foods and thus higher priced. However, they may be just as economical in the long run, because studies have shown that it takes less of the higher-quality foods to maintain a dog.

Comparing the various types of food—dry, canned and semi-moist—dry foods contain the least amount of water and canned foods the most. Proportionately, dry foods are the most calorie- and nutrient-dense, which means that you need more of a canned food product to supply the same amount of nutrition. In households with breeds of different sizes, the canned/dry/semi-moist question can be of special importance. Larger breeds obviously eat more than smaller ones and thus generally do better on dry foods, but smaller breeds do fine on canned foods and require "small bite" formulations to protect their small mouths and teeth if fed only dry foods. So if you have breeds of different sizes in your household, consider both your own preferences and what your dogs like to eat, but, as a rule of thumb, think canned for the little guys and dry or semi-moist for everyone else. You may find success mixing the food types as well. Water is important for all dogs, but even more so for those fed dry foods, as there is no high water content in their food.

There are strict controls that regulate the nutritional content of dog food, and a food has to meet the minimum requirements in order to be considered "complete and balanced." It is important that you choose such a food for your dog, so check the label to be sure that your chosen food meets the requirements. If not, look for a food that clearly states on the label that it is formulated to be complete and balanced for your dog's particular stage of life.

Recommendations for amounts to feed will also be indicated on the label. You should also ask your vet about proper food portions, and you will keep an eye on your dog's condition to see whether the recommended amounts are adequate. If he becomes over- or underweight, you will need to make adjustments; this also would be a good time to consult your vet.

The food label may also make feeding suggestions, such as whether moistening a dry-food product is recommended. Sometimes a splash of water will make the food more palatable for the dog and even enhance the flavor. Don't be overwhelmed by the many factors that go into feeding your dog. Manufacturers of complete and balanced foods make it easy, and once you find the right food and amounts for your Australian Terrier, his daily feeding will be a matter of routine.

Don't Forget the Water!

For a dog, it's always time for a drink! Regardless of what type of food he eats, there's no doubt that he needs plenty of water. Fresh cold water, in a clean bowl, should be freely available to your dog at all times. There are special circumstances, such as during puppy housebreaking, when you will want to monitor your pup's water intake so that you will be able to predict when he will need to relieve himself, but water must be available to him nonetheless. Water is essential for hydration and proper body function just as it is in humans.

You will get to know how much your dog typically drinks in a day. Of course, in the heat or if exercising vigorously, he will be more thirsty and will drink more. However, if he begins to drink noticeably more water for no apparent reason, this could signal any of various problems, and you are advised to consult your vet.

Water is the best drink for dogs. Some owners are tempted to give milk from time to time or to moisten dry food with milk, but dogs do not have the enzymes necessary to digest the lactose in milk, which is much different from the milk that nursing puppies receive. Therefore, stick with clean fresh water to quench your dog's thirst, and always have it readily available to him.

EXERCISE

We all know the importance of exercise for humans, so it should come as no surprise that it is essential for our canine friends as well. Now, regardless of your own level of fitness, get ready to assume the role of personal trainer for your dog. It's not as hard as it sounds, and it will have health benefits for you, too.

The easiest way to exercise your Aussie? Go for a walk!

Just as with anything else you do with your dog, you must set a routine for his exercise. It's the same as your daily morning run before work or never missing the 7 p.m. aerobics class. If you plan it and get into the habit of actually doing it, it will become just another part of your day. Think of it as making daily exercise appointments with your dog, and stick to your schedule.

As a rule, dogs in normal health should have at least half an hour of activity each day. Dogs with health or orthopedic problems may have specific limitations, so their exercise plans are best devised with the help of a vet. For healthy dogs, there are many ways to fit 30 minutes of activity into your day. Depending on your schedule, you may plan a 15-minute walk or activity session in the morning and again in the evening, or do it all at once in a half-hour session each day. Walking is the most popular way to exercise a dog (it's good for you, too!); other suggestions include retrieving games, jogging and disc-catching or other active games with his toys. If you have a safe body of water nearby and a dog that likes to swim, swimming is an excellent form of exercise for dogs, putting no stress on their frames.

On that note, some precautions should be taken with a puppy's exercise. During his first year, when he is growing and developing, your Australian Terrier should not be subject to stressful activity that stresses his body. Short walks at a comfortable pace and play sessions in the yard are good for a growing pup, and his exercise can be increased as he grows up.

For overweight dogs, dietary changes and activity will help the goal of weight loss. (Sound familiar?) While they should of course be encouraged to be active, remember not to overdo it, as the excess weight is already putting strain on his vital organs and bones. As for highly active dogs, some of them never seem to tire! They will enjoy time spent with their owners doing things together.

Regardless of your dog's condition and activity level, exercise offers benefits to all dogs and owners. Consider the fact that dogs who are kept active are more stimulated both physically and mentally, meaning that they are less likely to become bored and lapse into destructive behavior. Also consider the benefits of one-on-one time with your dog every day, continually strengthening the bond between the two of you. Furthermore, exercising together will improve health and longevity for both of you. You both need exercise, and now you and your dog have a workout partner and motivator!

TWO'S COMPANY

One surefire method of increasing your adult dog's exercise plan is to adopt a second dog. If your dog is well socialized, he should take to his new canine pal in no time and soon the two will be giving each other lots of activity and exercise as they play, romp and explore together. Most owners agree that two dogs are hardly much more work than one. If you cannot afford a second dog, get together with a friend or neighbor who has a well-trained dog. Your dog will definitely enjoy the company of a new four-legged playmate.

Even the active Aussie will get tired and let you know when he's ready to come in for a rest.

GROOMING YOUR AUSSIE

Do understand before purchasing your Aussie that this is a breed with a coat that will need some maintenance, whether you have a dog for the show ring or one that is a household pet. Think of it in terms of your child—you bathe your youngster, comb his hair and put a clean set of clothes on him. The end product is that you have a child that smells good and looks nice, and that you enjoy having in your company. It is the same with your dog—keep the dog brushed, cleaned and trimmed, and you will find it a pleasure to be in his company. However, it will require some effort to do this.

The Aussie is a double-coated dog. There is a dense, thick undercoat that protects the dog in all kinds of weather and there is a harsh outer coat. Coat care for the pet Aussie can be much different from and easier than the coat care for a show dog. The vast majority of Aussie fanciers have dogs as pets only, and they should not expect to maintain a show coat.

Pet Versus Show Grooming

If you are planning to show your Australian Terrier, you will be well served if you purchase your puppy from a reputable breeder who grooms and shows dogs. If so, this is the individual to see for grooming lessons to learn how to get your dog ready for the show ring. Grooming for the show is an art, and an art that cannot be learned in a few months. Furthermore, it is very difficult, but not impossible, to learn it from a book.

The primary difference between the pet and show Aussie coat is that the show dog will have a dense undercoat and, on top of it, he will have a tidy, harsh coat. With the proper coat, the dog presents a smartness in the ring that can be hard to beat. This coat can only be acquired by stripping the body coat, twice a year, with a stripping knife or by hand. This all takes skill, time and interest in order to do it well.

Pet grooming is different from grooming for the show ring, and you will not have the harsh, tidy coat of the show Aussie; instead, you will have a neat, clean and trimmed dog that will still look like a handsome Australian Terrier.

What You Will Need

You will need some tools if you are going to do your own grooming. First, you will need a grooming table, something sturdy with a rubber mat covering the top. You will also need a grooming arm or a "hanger." (You can use a table in your laundry room with an eye hook in the ceiling for holding the leash.) Your dog will now be comfortable, even if confined, and you will be able to work on the dog. Grooming is a very difficult and frustrating job if you try to groom without a table and a grooming arm.

To work on the dog's coat, you will need a metal comb, a slicker brush, a good sharp pair of scissors and a toenail trimmer. If you are going to attempt hand stripping, you will need a stripping knife as well.

Maintaining the Coat

To start, set your dog on the table and put the leash around his neck. Have the leash up behind the ears and have the leash taut when you fasten it to your eye hook. Do not walk away and leave your dog unattended, as he can jump off the table and be left dangling from the leash with his feet scrambling around in the air, possibly injuring himself and definitely scaring himself.

Take your slicker brush and brush out the entire coat. Brush the whiskers toward the nose, brush the body hair toward the tail and brush the tail up toward the tip of the tail. Brush the leg furnishings up toward the body and brush the chest hair outwards from under the throat to the shoulders; this will give you the bib-like ruff. Hold the dog up by the front legs and gently brush the stomach hair, first toward the head and then back toward the rear. For cleanliness, you may want to take your scissors and trim the area around the penis; with the girls, trim some of the hair around the vulva.

Now that your dog is brushed out, comb through the coat with your metal comb. By now you have removed a fair amount of

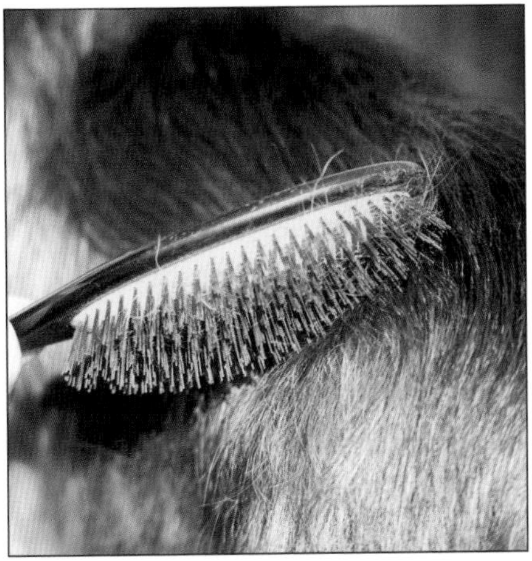

Begin grooming by brushing out the Australian Terrier's coat thoroughly, using a bristle brush or a slicker brush.

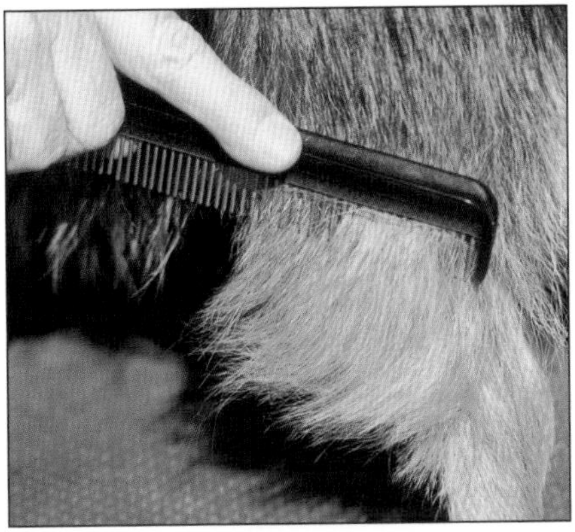

The metal comb helps to straighten the hair after brushing, locating and removing any mats that may have formed in the coat.

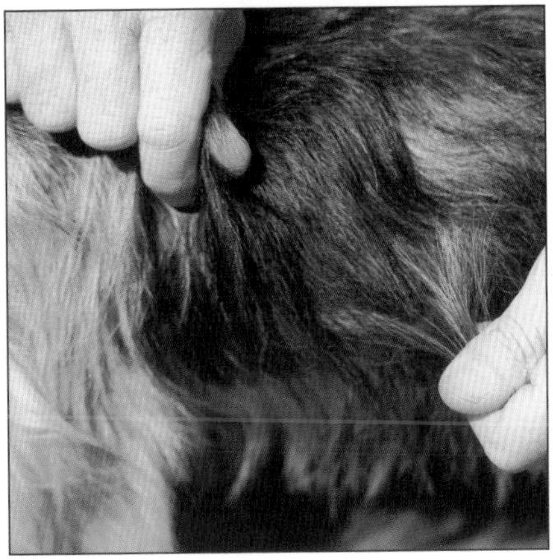

After brushing and combing, hand stripping will remove dead long hairs from the coat. Your breeder or a professional groomer can show you the proper way to approach this technique.

dead hair and your dog will already be looking better. You may find some small mats, and these can be worked out with your fingers or your comb. If you brush your dog out every week or so, you will not have too much of a problem with mats.

When you find that the coat is separating, you should be prepared to do some hand stripping. This is the process of pulling out the dead long coat in the direction in which it lies. It is best to have a stripping knife for this process, and it is by far better if your breeder or someone else can show you how this is to be done properly. Of course, you can clip your dog down, leaving a trimmed head, and within 8 to 10 weeks your dog will have a soft, but nice, coat.

Find a good picture of an Australian Terrier in show trim. This will give you an idea of how the dog should look when he is groomed. If this is your first experience, you may be a bit clumsy, but the hair will grow back in a short time. The finished product may not be quite what you had expected, but expertise will come with experience and you will soon be very proud of your efforts.

If you have grooming problems, you can take your dog to the professional groomer for the first few times. (Of course, you can eliminate all of the grooming for yourself, except for the weekly brushing, if you take your dog to the groomer every three months.) Just remember, many pet owners can do a much better job groom-

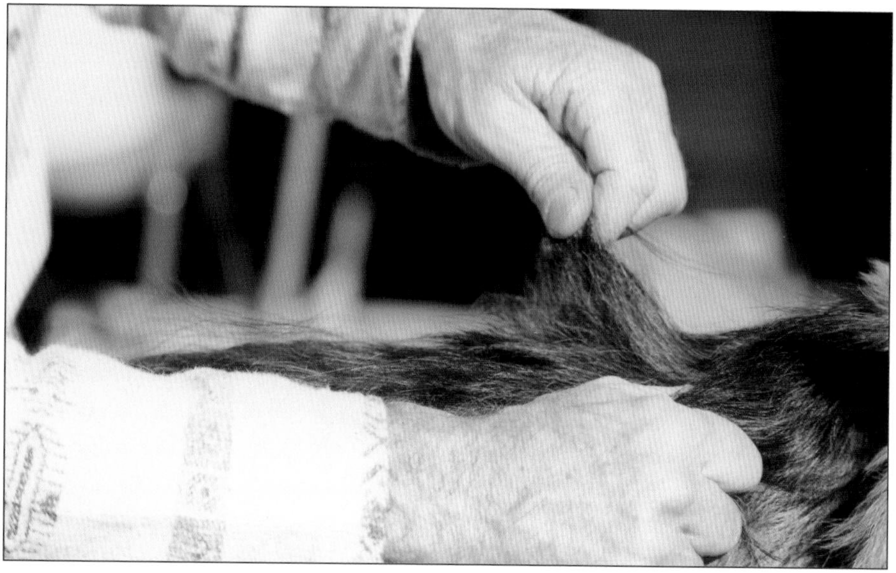

Hand stripping is required to maintain the Australian Terrier's characteristic harsh appearance and feel. When the procedure is done properly, the dog does not experience discomfort.

ing their dogs than some professional groomers.

To wrap it up, your pet should be brushed weekly and bathed as needed. Trim the toenails every month or so and plan to either hand-strip or clip the dog as needed. Follow this plan and your dog will be clean and tidy, looking like a proper Australian Terrier, whether in show coat or pet trim, or somewhere in between.

Bathing

In general, dogs need to be bathed only a few times a year, possibly more often if your dog gets into something messy or if he starts to smell like a dog. Show dogs may be bathed more frequently, according to the show schedule, although this depends on the owner. Bathing too frequently can have negative effects on the skin and coat, removing natural oils, causing dryness and softening the proper harsh coat texture.

If you give your dog his first bath when he is young, he will become accustomed to the process. Wrestling a dog into the tub or chasing a freshly shampooed dog who has escaped from the bath will be no fun! Most dogs don't naturally enjoy their baths, but you at least want yours to cooperate with you.

Before bathing the dog, have the items you'll need close at hand. First, decide where you will bathe the dog. You should have a tub or basin with a non-slip surface. Puppies can even be bathed in a sink. In warm weather, some like to use a portable pool in the yard, although you'll want to make sure your dog doesn't head for the nearest dirt pile following his bath! You will also need a hose or shower spray to wet the coat thoroughly, a shampoo formulated for dogs and a few absorbent towels. Human shampoos are too harsh for dogs' coats and will dry them out.

WATER SHORTAGE

No matter how well behaved your dog is, bathing is always a project! Nothing can substitute for a good warm bath, but owners do have the option of giving their dogs "dry" baths. Pet shops sell excellent products, in both powder and spray forms, designed for spot-cleaning your dog. These dry shampoos are convenient for touch-up jobs when you don't have the time to bathe your dog in the traditional way.

Muddy feet, messy behinds and smelly coats can be spot-cleaned and deodorized with a "wet-nap"-style cleaner. On those days when your dog insists on rolling in fresh goose droppings and there's no time for a bath, a spot bath can save the day. These pre-moistened wipes are also handy for other grooming needs like wiping faces, ears and eyes and freshening tails and behinds.

Before wetting the dog, give him a brush-through to remove any dead hair, dirt and mats. Make sure he is at ease in the tub and have the water at a comfortable temperature. Begin bathing by wetting the coat all the way down to the skin. Massage in the shampoo, keeping it away from his face and eyes. Rinse him thoroughly, again avoiding the eyes and ears, as you don't want to get water into the ear canals. A thorough rinsing is important, as shampoo residue is drying and itchy to the dog. After rinsing, wrap him in a towel to absorb the initial moisture. You can finish towel-drying him, brushing through as the coat dries. You should keep the dog indoors and away from drafts until he is completely dry.

Nail Clipping

Having his nails trimmed is not on many dogs' lists of favorite things to do. With this in mind, you will need to accustom your puppy to the procedure at a young age so that he will sit still (well, as still as he can) for his pedicures. Long nails can cause the dog's feet to spread, which is not good for him; likewise, long nails can hurt if they unintentionally scratch, not good for you!

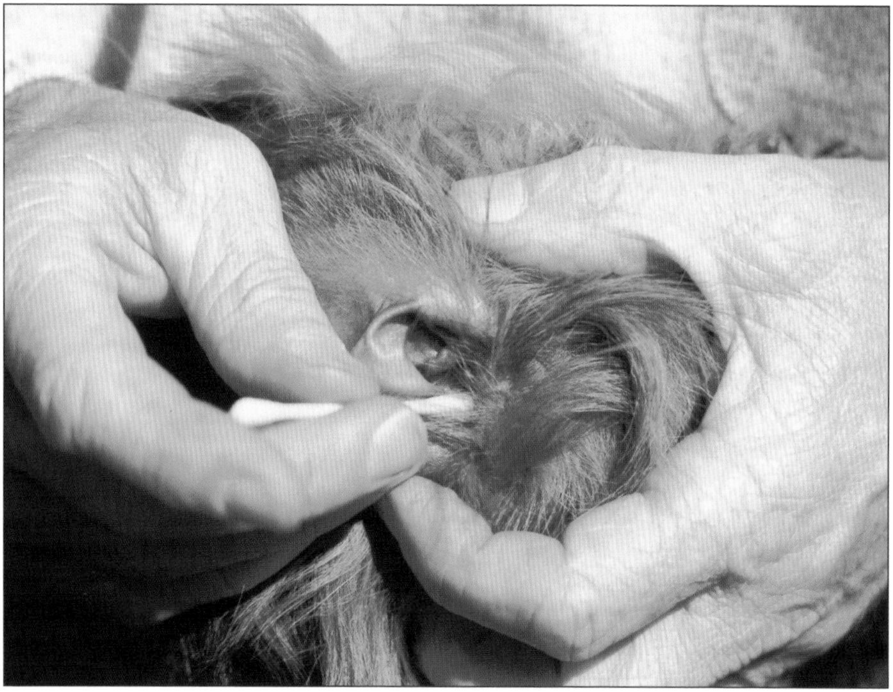

The Australian Terrier's ears should be cleaned with a soft cotton wipe and a specially made ear cleaner. Probing the ear with a cotton swab, shown here, is not advised, as you may cause harm to the inner ear.

Some dogs' nails are worn down naturally by regular walking on hard surfaces, so the frequency with which you clip depends on your individual dog. Look at his nails from time to time and clip as needed; a good way to know when it's time for a trim is if you hear your dog clicking as he walks across the floor.

There are several types of nail clippers and even electric nail-grinding tools made for dogs; first we'll discuss using the clipper. To start, have your clipper ready and some doggie treats on hand. You want your pup to view his nail-clipping sessions in a positive light, and what better way to convince him than with food? You may want to enlist the help of an assistant to comfort the pup and offer treats as you concentrate on the clipping itself. The guillotine-type clipper is thought of by many as the easiest type to use; the nail tip is inserted into the opening, and blades on the top and bottom snip it off in one clip.

Start by grasping the pup's paw; a little pressure on the foot pad causes the nail to extend, making it easier to clip. Clip off a little at a time. If you can see the "quick," which is a blood vessel that runs through each nail, you will know how much to trim, as you do not want to cut into the quick. On that note, if you do cut the quick, which will cause bleeding, you can stem the flow of blood with a styptic pencil or other clotting agent. If you mistakenly nip the quick, do not panic or fuss, as this will cause the pup to be afraid. Simply reassure the pup, stop the bleeding and move on to the next nail. Don't be discouraged; you will become a professional canine pedicurist with practice.

Frequent walks on pavement and sidewalks will wear down a dog's nails, making nail clipping needed less frequently.

You may or may not be able to see the quick, so it's best to just clip off a small bit at a time. If you see a dark dot in the center of the nail, this is the quick and your cue to stop clipping. Tell the puppy he's a "good boy" and offer a piece of treat with each nail. You can also use nail-clipping time to examine the footpads, making sure that they are not dry and cracked and that nothing has become embedded in them.

The nail grinder, the other choice, is many owners' first

choice. Accustoming the puppy to the sound of the grinder and sensation of the buzz presents fewer challenges than the clipper, and there's no chance of cutting through the quick. Use the grinder on a low setting and always talk soothingly to your dog. He won't mind his salon visit, and he'll have nicely polished nails as well.

Ear Cleaning

While keeping your dog's ears clean unfortunately will not cause him to "hear" your commands any better, it will protect him from ear infection and ear-mite infestation. In addition, a dog's ears are vulnerable to waxy build-up and to collecting foreign matter from the outdoors. Look in your dog's ears regularly to ensure that they look pink, clean and otherwise healthy. Even if they look fine, an odor in the ears signals a problem and means it's time to call the vet.

A dog's ears should be cleaned regularly; once a week is suggested, and you can do this along with your regular brushing. Using a cotton ball or pad and never probing into the ear canal, wipe the ear gently. You can use an ear-cleansing liquid or powder available from your vet or pet-supply store; alternatively, you might prefer to use homemade solutions with ingredients like one part white vinegar and one part hydrogen peroxide. Ask your vet about home remedies before you attempt to concoct something on your own!

Keep your dog's ears free of excess hair by plucking it as needed. If done gently, this will be painless for the dog. Look for wax, brown droppings (a sign of ear mites), redness or any other abnormalities. At the first sign of a problem, contact your vet so that he can prescribe an appropriate medication.

SCOOTING HIS BOTTOM

Here's a doggy problem that many owners tend to neglect. If your dog is scooting his rear end around the carpet, he probably is experiencing anal-sac impaction or blockage. The anal sacs are the two grape-sized glands on either side of the dog's vent. The dog cannot empty these glands, which become filled with a foul-smelling material. The dog may attempt to lick the area to relieve the pressure. He may also rub his anus on your walls, furniture or floors.

Don't neglect your dog's rear end during grooming sessions. By squeezing both sides of the anus with a soft cloth, you can express some of the material in the sacs. If the material is pasty and thick, you likely will need the assistance of a veterinarian. Vets know how to express the glands and can show you how to do it correctly without hurting the dog or spraying yourself with foul liquid.

Eye Care

During grooming sessions, pay extra attention to the condition of your dog's eyes. If the area around the eyes is soiled or if tear staining has occurred, there are various cleaning agents made especially for this purpose. Look at the dog's eyes to make sure no debris has entered; dogs who spend time outdoors are especially prone to this, so be aware of your Aussie's eyes.

The signs of an eye infection are obvious: mucus, redness, puffiness, scabs or other signs of irritation. If your dog's eyes become infected, the vet will likely prescribe an antibiotic ointment for treatment. If you notice signs of more serious problems, such as opacities in the eye, which usually indicate cataracts, consult the vet at once. Taking time to pay attention to your dog's eyes will alert you in the early stages of any problem so that you can get your dog treatment as soon as possible. You could save your dog's sight!

IDENTIFICATION AND TRAVEL

ID for Your Dog

You love your Australian Terrier and want to keep him safe. Of course, you take every precaution to prevent his escaping from the yard or becoming lost or stolen. You have a sturdy high fence and you always keep your dog on lead when out and about in public places. If your dog is not properly identified, however, you are overlooking a major aspect of his safety. We hope to never be in a situation where our dog is

PRESERVING THOSE PEARLY WHITES

What do you treasure more than the smile of your beloved canine pal? Brushing your dog's teeth is just as important as brushing your own. Neglecting your dog's teeth can lead to tooth loss, periodontal disease and inflamed gums, not to mention bad breath. Can you find the time to brush your dog's teeth every day? If not, you should do so once a week at the very least, though every day is truly the ideal. Your vet should give your dog a thorough dental examination during his annual check-ups.

Pet shops sell terrific tooth-care devices, including specially designed toothbrushes, yummy toothpastes and finger-model brushes. You can use a human toothbrush with soft bristles, but never use human toothpastes, which can damage the dog's enamel. Baking soda is an alternative to doggy toothpastes, but your dog will be more receptive to canine toothpastes with the flavor of liver or hamburger. Make tooth care fun for your dog. Let him think that you're "horsing around" with his mouth. When brushing the dog's teeth, begin with the largest teeth (the canines) and proceed back toward the molars.

Use your dog's crate to travel safely with your Australian Terrier in the car. This is the safest option when traveling with your dog.

PET OR STRAY?
Besides the obvious benefit of providing your contact information to whoever finds your lost dog, an ID tag makes your dog more approachable and more likely to be recovered. A strange dog wandering the neighborhood without a collar and tags will look like a stray, while the collar and tags indicate that the dog is someone's pet. Even if the ID tags become detached from the collar, the collar alone will make a person more likely to pick up the dog.

missing, but we should practice prevention in the unfortunate case that this happens; identification greatly increases the chances of your dog's being returned to you

There are several ways to identify your dog. First, the traditional dog tag should be a staple in your dog's wardrobe, attached to his everyday collar. Tags can be made of sturdy plastic and various metals and should include your contact information so that a person who finds the dog can get in touch with you right away to arrange his return. Many people today enjoy the wide range of decorative tags available, so have fun and create a tag to match your dog's personality. Of course, it is important that the tag stays on the collar, so have a secure "O" ring attachment; you also can explore the type of tag that slides right onto the collar.

In addition to the ID tag, which every dog should wear even if identified by another method, two other forms of identification have become popular: microchipping and tattooing. In microchipping, a tiny scannable chip is painlessly inserted under the dog's skin. The number is registered to you so that, if your lost dog turns up at a clinic or shelter, the chip can be scanned to retrieve your contact information.

The advantage of the microchip is that it is a permanent form of ID, but there are some factors to consider. Several different companies make microchips, and not all are compatible with the others' scan-

Your Aussie will jump at the chance to explore wherever you go, so be sure to keep him safely on lead while traveling and making pitstops.

Depending on your individual dog, staying at a boarding kennel may be either a stressful experience or an enjoyable vacation.

ning devices. It's best to find a company with a universal microchip that can be read by scanners made by other companies as well. It won't do any good to have the dog chipped if the information cannot be retrieved. Also, not every humane society, shelter and clinic is equipped with a scanner, although more and more facilities are equipping themselves. In fact, many shelters microchip dogs that they adopt out to new homes.

Humane societies and veterinary clinics offer microchipping service, which is usually very affordable. Because the microchip is not visible to the eye, the dog must wear a tag that states that he is microchipped so that whoever picks him up will know to have him scanned. He of course also should have a tag with contact information in case his chip cannot be read.

Though less popular than microchipping, tattooing is another permanent method of ID for dogs. Most vets perform this service, and there are also clinics that perform dog tattooing. This is also an affordable procedure and one that will not cause much discomfort for the dog. It is best to put the tattoo in a visible area, such as the ear, to deter theft. It is sad to say that there are cases of dogs' being stolen and sold to research laboratories, but such laboratories will not accept tattooed dogs.

To ensure that the tattoo is effective in aiding your dog's return to you, the tattoo number must be registered with a national organiza-

YOUR PACK ANIMAL

If you are bringing your dog along with you on a vacation, here's a list of the things you want to pack for him:

- leashes (conventional and retractable)
- collar with ID tag
- dog food and bottled water
- grooming tools
- flea and tick sprays
- crate and crate pad
- pooper-scooper and plastic bags
- toys and treats
- towels and paper towels
- first-aid kit
- dog license and rabies certificate

tion. That way, when someone finds a tattooed dog a phone call to the registry will quickly match the dog with his owner.

Hit the Road

Car travel with your Australian Terrier may be limited to necessity only, such as trips to the vet, or you may bring your dog along almost everywhere you go. This will depend much on your individual dog and how he reacts to rides in the car. You can begin desensitizing your dog to car travel as a pup so that it's something that he's used to. Still, some dogs suffer from motion sickness. Your vet may prescribe a medication for this if trips in the car pose a problem for your dog. At the very least, you will need to get him to the vet, so he will need to tolerate these trips with the least amount of hassle possible.

Start taking your pup on short trips, maybe just around the block to start. If he is fine with short trips, lengthen your rides a little at a time. Start to take him on your errands or just for drives around town. By this time it will be easy to tell whether your dog is a born traveler or would prefer staying at home when you are on the road.

Of course, safety is a concern for dogs in the car. First, he must travel securely, not left loose to roam about the car where he could be injured or distract the driver. A young pup can be held by a passenger initially but should soon graduate to a travel crate, which can be the same crate he uses in the home. Other options include a car harness (like a seat belt for dogs) and partitioning the back of the car with a gate made for this purpose.

Bring along what you will need for the dog. He should wear his collar and ID tags, of course, and you should bring his leash, water (and food if a long trip) and clean-up materials for potty breaks and in case of motion sickness. Always keep your dog on his leash when you make stops, and never leave him alone in the car. Many a dog has died from the heat inside a closed car; this does not take much time at all. A dog left alone inside a car can also be a target for thieves.

DOGGONE!

Wendy Ballard is the editor and publisher of the *DogGone*™ newsletter, which comes out bi-monthly and features fun articles by dog owners who love to travel with their dogs. The newsletter includes information about fun places to go with your dogs, including popular vacation spots, dog-friendly hotels, parks, campgrounds, resorts, etc., as well as interesting activities to do with your dog, such as flyball, agility and much more. You can subscribe to the publication by contacting the publisher at PO Box 651155, Vero Beach, FL 32965-1155.

TRAINING YOUR
AUSTRALIAN TERRIER

BASIC TRAINING PRINCIPLES: PUPPY VS. ADULT

There's a big difference between training an adult dog and training a young puppy. With a young puppy, everything is new. At eight to ten weeks of age, he will be experiencing many things, and he has nothing with which to compare these experiences. Up to this point, he has been with his dam and littermates, not one-on-one with people except in his interactions with his breeder and visitors to the litter.

Treats are the key to training a dog to obey commands. You can count on your Australian Terrier's undivided attention when you are dangling a tasty morsel of cheese or chicken over his head.

When you first bring the puppy home, he is eager to please you. This means that he accepts doing things your way. During the next couple of months, he will absorb the basis of everything he needs to know for the rest of his life. This early age is even referred to as the "sponge" stage. After that, for the next 18 months, it's up to you to reinforce good manners by building on the foundation that you've established. Once your puppy is reliable in basic commands and behavior and has reached the appropriate age, you may gradually introduce him to some of the interesting sports, games and activities available to pet owners and their dogs.

Raising your puppy is a family affair. Each member of the family must know what rules to set forth for the puppy and how to use the same one-word commands to mean exactly the same thing every time. Even if yours is a large family, one person will soon be considered by the pup to be the leader, the Alpha person in his pack, the "boss" who must be obeyed. Often that highly regarded person turns out to be the one who feeds the puppy. Food ranks very high on the puppy's list of important things! That's why your puppy is rewarded with small treats along with verbal praise when he responds to you correctly. As the puppy learns to do what you want him to do, the food rewards are gradually eliminated and only the praise remains. If you were to keep up with the food treats, you could have two problems on your hands—an obese dog and a beggar.

Training begins the minute your Australian Terrier puppy steps through the doorway of your home, so don't make the mistake of putting the puppy on the floor and telling him by your actions to "Go for it! Run wild!" Even if this is your first puppy, you must act as if you know what you're doing: be the boss. An uncertain pup may be terrified to move, while a bold one will be ready to take you at your word and start plotting to destroy the house! Before you collected your puppy, you decided where his own special place would be, and that's where to put him when you first arrive home. Give him a house tour after he has investigated his area and had a nap and a bathroom "pit stop."

It's worth mentioning here that if you've adopted an adult dog that is completely trained to your liking, lucky you! You're off the hook! However, if that dog

Children and dogs that grow up together form a special bond of closeness and friendship.

LEADER OF THE PACK

Canines are pack animals. They live according to pack rules, and every pack has only one leader. Guess what? That's you! To establish your position of authority, lay down the rules and be fair and good-natured in all your dealings with your dog. He will consider young children as his littermates, but the one who trains him, who feeds him, who grooms him, who expects him to come into line, that's his leader. And he who leads must be obeyed.

spent his life up to this point in a kennel, or even in a good home but without any real training, be prepared to tackle the job ahead. A dog three years of age or older with no previous training cannot be blamed for not knowing what he was never taught. While the dog is trying to understand and learn your rules, at the same time he has to unlearn many of his previously self-taught habits and general view of the world.

"SCHOOL" MODE

When is your puppy ready for a lesson? Maybe not always when you are. Attempting training with treats just before his mealtime is asking for disaster. Notice what times of day he performs best and make that Fido's school time.

Working with a professional trainer will speed up your progress with an adopted adult dog. You'll need patience, too. Some new rules may be close to impossible for the dog to accept. After all, he's been successful so far by doing everything his way! (Patience again.) He may agree with your instruction for a few days and then slip back into his old ways, so you must be just as consistent and understanding in your teaching as you would be with a puppy. (More patience needed yet again!) Your dog has to learn to pay attention to your voice, your family, the daily routine, new smells, new sounds and, in some cases, even a new climate.

One of the most important things to find out about a newly adopted adult dog is his reaction to children (yours and others), strangers and your friends, and how he acts upon meeting other dogs. If he was not socialized with dogs as a puppy, this could be a major problem. This does not mean that he's a "bad" dog, a vicious dog or an aggressive dog; rather, it means that he has no idea how to read another dog's body language. There's no way for him to tell whether the other dog is a friend or foe. Survival instinct takes over, telling him to attack first and ask questions later. This definitely calls for professional help and, even then, may not be a behavior that can be corrected 100% reliably (or even at all). If you have a puppy, this is why it is so very important to introduce your young puppy properly to other puppies and "dog-friendly" adult dogs.

HOUSE-TRAINING

Dogs are tactility-oriented when it comes to house-training. In other words, they respond to the surface on which they are given approval to eliminate. The choice is yours (the dog's version is in parentheses): The lawn (including the neighbors' lawns)? A bare patch of earth under a tree (where people like to sit and relax in the summertime)? Concrete steps or patio (all sidewalks, garages and basement floors)? The curbside (watch out for cars)? A small area of crushed stone in a corner of the yard (mine!)? The latter is the best choice if you can manage it, because it will remain strictly for the dog's use and is easy to keep clean.

A happy trio of Aussies cuddling up with friends. Well-trained, well-socialized dogs rub off on each other.

You can start out with paper-training indoors and switch over to an outdoor surface as the puppy matures and gains control over his need to eliminate. For the nay-sayers, don't worry—this won't mean that the dog will soil on every piece of newspaper lying around the house. You are training him to go outside, remember? Starting out by paper-training often is the only choice for a city dog.

WHEN YOUR PUPPY'S "GOT TO GO"

Your puppy's need to relieve himself is seemingly non-stop, but signs of improvement will be seen each week. From 8 to 10 weeks old, the puppy will have to be taken outside every time he wakes up, about 10–15 minutes after every meal and after every period

> **SHOULD WE ENROLL?**
> If you have the means and the time, you should definitely take your dog to obedience classes. Begin with Puppy Kindergarten Classes in which puppies of all sizes learn basic lessons while getting the opportunity to meet and greet each other; it's as much about socialization as it is about good manners. What you learn in class you can practice at home. And if you goof up in practice, you'll get help in the next session.

EXTRA! EXTRA!

The headlines read: "Puppy Piddles Here!" Breeders commonly use newspapers to line their whelping pens, so puppies learn to associate newspapers with relieving themselves. Do not use newspapers to line your pup's crate, as this will signal to your puppy that it is OK to urinate in his crate. If you choose to paper-train your puppy, you will layer newspapers on a section of the floor near the door he uses to go outside. You should encourage the puppy to use the papers to relieve himself, and bring him there whenever you see him getting ready to go. Little by little, you will reduce the size of the newspaper-covered area so that the puppy will learn to relieve himself "on the other side of the door."

of play—all day long, from first thing in the morning until his bedtime! That's a total of ten or more trips per day to teach the puppy where it's okay to relieve himself. With that schedule in mind, you can see that house-training a young puppy is not a part-time job. It requires someone to be home all day.

If that seems overwhelming or impossible, do a little planning. For example, plan to pick up your puppy at the start of a vacation period. If you can't get home in the middle of the day, plan to hire a dog-sitter or ask a neighbor to come over to take the pup outside, feed him his lunch and then take him out again about ten or so minutes after he's eaten. Also make arrangements with that or another person to be your "emergency" contact if you have to stay late on the job. Remind yourself—repeatedly—that this hectic schedule improves as the puppy gets older.

Home within a Home

Your Australian Terrier puppy needs to be confined to one secure, puppy-proof area when no one is able to watch his every move. Generally the kitchen is the place of choice because the floor is washable. Likewise, it's a busy family area that will accustom the pup to a variety of noises, everything from pots and pans to the telephone, blender and dishwasher. He will also be enchanted by the smell of your cooking (and will never be critical when you burn something). An exercise pen (also called an "ex-pen," a puppy version of a

Canine Development Schedule

It is important to understand how and at what age a puppy develops into adulthood. If you are a puppy owner, consult the following Canine Development Schedule to determine the stage of development your puppy is currently experiencing. This knowledge will help you as you work with the puppy in the weeks and months ahead.

Period	Age	Characteristics
First to Third	Birth to Seven Weeks	Puppy needs food, sleep and warmth and responds to simple and gentle touching. Needs mother for security and disciplining. Needs littermates for learning and interacting with other dogs. Pup learns to function within a pack and learns pack order of dominance. Begin socializing pup with adults and children for short periods. Pup begins to become aware of his environment.
Fourth	Eight to Twelve Weeks	Brain is fully developed. Pup needs socializing with outside world. Remove from mother and littermates. Needs to change from canine pack to human pack. Human dominance necessary. Fear period occurs between 8 and 12 weeks. Avoid fright and pain.
Fifth	Thirteen to Sixteen Weeks	Training and formal obedience should begin. Less association with other dogs, more with people, places, situations. Period will pass easily if you remember this is pup's change-to-adolescence time. Be firm and fair. Flight instinct prominent. Permissiveness and over-disciplining can do permanent damage. Praise for good behavior.
Juvenile	Four to Eight Months	Another fear period about 7 to 8 months of age. It passes quickly, but be cautious of fright and pain. Sexual maturity reached. Dominant traits established. Dog should understand sit, down, come and stay by now.

Note: These are approximate time frames. Allow for individual differences in puppies.

LEASH TRAINING

House-training and leash training go hand in hand, literally. When taking your puppy outside to do his business, lead him there on his leash. Unless an emergency potty run is called for, do not whisk the puppy up into your arms and take him outside. If you have a fenced yard, you have the advantage of letting the puppy loose to go out, but it's better to put the dog on the leash and take him to his designated place in the yard until he is reliably house-trained. Taking the puppy for a walk is the best way to house-train a dog. The dog will associate the walk with his time to relieve himself, and the exercise of walking stimulates the dog's bowels and bladder. Dogs that are not trained to relieve themselves on a walk may hold it until they get back home, which of course defeats half the purpose of the walk.

playpen) within the room of choice is an excellent means of confinement for a young pup. He can see out and has a certain amount of space in which to run about, but he is safe from dangerous things like electrical cords, heating units, trash baskets or open kitchen-supply cabinets. Place the pen where the puppy will not get a blast of heat or air conditioning.

In the pen, you can put a few toys, his bed (which can be his crate if the dimensions of pen and crate are compatible) and a few layers of newspaper in one small corner, just in case. A water bowl can be hung at a convenient height on the side of the ex-pen so it won't become a splashing pool for an innovative puppy. His food dish can go on the floor, by the water bowl.

Crates are something that pet owners are at last getting used to for their dogs. Wild or domestic canines have always preferred to sleep in den-like safe spots, and that is exactly what the crate provides. How often have you seen adult dogs that choose to sleep under a table or chair even though they have full run of the house? It's the den connection.

In your "happy" voice, use the word "Crate" every time you put the pup into his den. If he's new to a crate, toss in a small biscuit for him to chase the first few times. At night, after he's been outside, he should sleep in his crate. The crate may be kept in his designated area at night or, if you want to be sure to hear those wake-up yips in the morning, put the crate in a corner of your bedroom. However, don't make any response whatsoever to whining or crying. If he's completely ignored, he'll settle down and get to sleep.

Good bedding for a young puppy is an old folded bath towel or an old blanket, something that is easily washable and disposable if necessary ("accidents" will happen!). Never put newspaper in the puppy's crate. Also, those old

Your Australian Terrier will welcome a wire crate with soft bedding, creating a cozy den all his own.

The Australian Terrier should be introduced to the house rules from the very beginning. If you do not want your adult Aussie to sit on your furniture, you cannot permit him to do so as a puppy.

ideas about adding a clock to replace his mother's heartbeat, or a hot-water bottle to replace her warmth, are just that—old ideas. The clock could drive the puppy nuts, and the hot-water bottle could end up as a very soggy waterbed! An extremely good breeder would have introduced your puppy to the crate by letting two pups sleep together for a couple of nights, followed by several nights alone. How thankful you will be if you found that breeder!

Safe toys in the pup's crate or area will keep him occupied, but monitor their condition closely. Discard any toys that show signs of being chewed to bits. Squeaky parts, bits of stuffing or plastic or any other small pieces can cause intestinal blockage or possibly choking if swallowed.

Progressing with Potty-Training

After you've taken your puppy out and he has relieved himself in the area you've selected, he can have some free time with the family as long as there is someone responsible for watching him. That doesn't mean just someone in the same room who is watching TV or busy on the computer, but one person who is doing nothing other than keeping an eye on the pup, playing with him on the floor and helping him understand his position in the pack.

This first taste of freedom will let you begin to set the house rules. If you don't want the dog on the furniture, now is the time to prevent his first attempts to jump up onto the couch. The word to use in this case is "Off," not "Down." "Down" is the word you will use to teach the down position, which is something entirely different.

Most corrections at this stage come in the form of simply distracting the puppy. Instead of

SOMEBODY TO BLAME

House-training a puppy can be frustrating for the puppy and the owner alike. The puppy does not instinctively understand the difference between defecating on the pavement outside and on the ceramic tile in the kitchen. He is confused and frightened by his human's exuberant reactions to his natural urges. The owner, arguably the more intelligent of the duo, is also frustrated that he cannot convince his puppy to obey his commands and instructions.

In frustration, the owner may struggle with the temptation to discipline the puppy, scold him or even strike him on the rear end. Shouting and smacking the puppy may make you feel better, but it will defeat your purpose in gaining your puppy's trust and respect. Don't blame your nine-week-old puppy. Blame yourself for not being 100% consistent in the puppy's lessons and routine. The lesson here is simple: try harder and your puppy will succeed.

telling him "No" for "Don't chew the carpet," distract the chomping puppy with a toy and he'll forget about the carpet.

As you are playing with the pup, do not forget to watch him closely and pay attention to his body language. Whenever you see him begin to circle or sniff, take

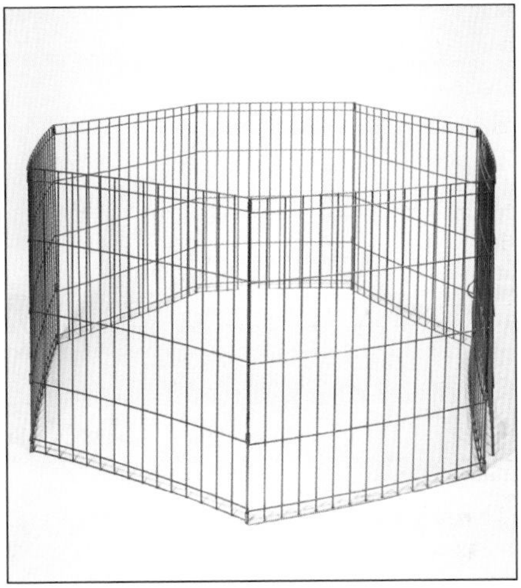

The "ex-pen" can be set up anywhere you need to provide your Aussie with an area of safe confinement.

the puppy outside to relieve himself. If you are paper-training, put him back into his confined area on the newspapers. In either case, praise him as he eliminates while he actually is in the act of relieving himself. Three seconds after he has finished is too late! You'll be praising him for running toward you, or picking up a toy or whatever he may be doing at that moment, and that's not what you want to be praising him for. Timing is a vital tool in all dog training. Use it.

Remove soiled newspapers immediately and replace them with clean ones. You may want to take a small piece of soiled paper and place it in the middle of the new clean papers, as the scent will attract him to that spot when it's time to go again. That scent attraction is why it's so important to clean up any messes made in

DAILY SCHEDULE

How many relief trips does your puppy need per day? A puppy up to the age of 14 weeks will need to go outside about 8 to 12 times per day! You will have to take the pup out any time he starts sniffing around the floor or turning in small circles, as well as after naps, meals, games and lessons or whenever he's released from his crate. Once the puppy is 14 to 22 weeks of age, he will require only 6 to 8 relief trips. At the ages of 22 to 32 weeks, the puppy will require about 5 to 7 trips. Adult dogs typically require 4 relief trips per day, in the morning, afternoon, evening and late at night.

Even getting the attention of two Aussies is a snap when there's a tasty morsel at stake.

the house by using a product specially made to eliminate the odor of dog urine and droppings. Regular household cleansers won't do the trick. Pet shops sell the best pet deodorizers. Invest in the largest container you can find!

Scent attraction eventually will lead your pup to his chosen spot outdoors; this is the basis of outdoor training. When you take your puppy outside to relieve himself, use a one-word command such as "Outside" or "Go-potty" (that's one word to the puppy!) as you pick him up and attach his leash. Then put him down in his area. If for any reason you can't carry him, snap the leash on quickly and lead him to his spot. Now comes the hard part—hard for you, that is. Just stand there until he urinates and defecates. Move him a few feet in one direction or another if he's just sitting there looking at you, but remember that this is neither playtime nor time for a walk. This is strictly a business trip! Then, as he circles and squats (remember your timing!), give him a quiet "Good dog" as praise. If you start to jump for joy, ecstatic over his performance, he'll do one of two things: either he will stop midstream, as it were, or he'll do it again for you—in the house—and expect you to be just as delighted!

POTTY COMMAND

Most dogs love to please their masters; there are no bounds to what dogs will do to make their owners happy. The potty command is a good example of this theory. If toileting on command makes the master happy, then more power to him. Puppies will obligingly piddle if it really makes their keepers smile. Some owners can be creative about which word they will use to command their dogs to relieve themselves. Some popular choices are "Potty," "Tinkle," "Piddle," "Let's go," "Hurry up" and "Toilet." Give the command every time your puppy goes into position and the puppy will begin to associate his business with the command.

Give him five minutes or so and, if he doesn't go in that time, take him back indoors to his confined area and try again in another ten minutes, or immediately if you see him sniffing and circling. By careful observation, you'll soon work out a successful schedule.

Accidents, by the way, are just that—accidents. Clean them up quickly and thoroughly, without comment, after the puppy has been taken outside to finish his business and then put back into his area or crate. If you witness an accident in progress, say "No!" in a stern voice and get the pup outdoors immediately. No punishment is needed. You and your puppy are just learning each other's language, and sometimes it's easy to miss a puppy's message. Chalk it up to experience and watch more closely from now on.

TEACHER'S PET

Dogs are individuals, not robots, with many traits basic to their breed. Some, bred to work alone, are independent thinkers; others rely on you to call the shots. If you have enrolled in a training class, your instructor can offer alternative methods of training based on your individual dog's instincts and personality. You may benefit from using a different type of collar or switching to a class with different kinds of dogs.

The scent instinct is what leads a pup to his relief area once he's used it a few times.

KEEPING THE PACK ORDERLY

Discipline is a form of training that brings order to life. For example, military discipline is what allows the soldiers in an army to work as one. Discipline is a form of teaching and, in dogs, is the basis of how the successful pack operates. Each member knows his place in the pack and all respect the leader, or Alpha dog. It is essential for your puppy that you establish this type of relationship, with you as the Alpha, or leader. It is a form of social coexistence that all canines recognize and accept. Discipline, therefore, is never to be confused with punishment. When you teach your puppy how you want him to behave, and he behaves properly and you praise him for it, you are disciplining him with a form of positive reinforcement.

For a dog, rewards come in the form of praise, a smile, a

Your Aussie must learn to get along with all members of his pack—even the feline ones!

cheerful tone of voice, a few friendly pats or a rub of the ears. Rewards are also small food treats. Obviously, that does not mean bits of regular dog food. Instead, treats are very small bits of special things like cheese or pieces of soft dog treats. The idea is to reward the dog with something very small that he can taste and swallow, providing instant positive reinforcement. If he has to take time to chew the treat, he will have forgotten what he did to earn it by the time he is finished!

Your puppy should never be physically punished. The displeasure shown on your face and in your voice is sufficient to signal to the pup that he has done something wrong. He wants to please everyone higher up on the social ladder, especially his leader, so a scowl and harsh voice will take care of the error. Growling out the word "Shame!" when the pup is caught in the act of doing something wrong is better than the repetitive "No." Some dogs hear "No" so often that they begin to think it's their name! By the way, do not use the dog's name when you're correcting him. His name is reserved to get his attention for something pleasant about to take place.

There are punishments that have nothing to do with you. For example, your dog may think that chasing cats is one reason for his existence. You can try to stop it as much as you like but without success, because it's such fun for the dog. But one good hissing, spitting, swipe of a cat's claws across the dog's nose will put an end to the game forever. Intervene only when your dog's eyeball is seriously at risk. Cat scratches can cause permanent damage to an innocent but annoying puppy.

BASIC PRINCIPLES OF DOG TRAINING

1. Start training early. A young puppy is ready, willing and able.
2. Timing is your all-important tool. Praise at the exact time that the dog responds correctly. Pay close attention.
3. Patience is almost as important as timing!
4. Repeat! The same word has to mean the same thing every time.
5. In the beginning, praise all correct behavior verbally, along with treats and petting.

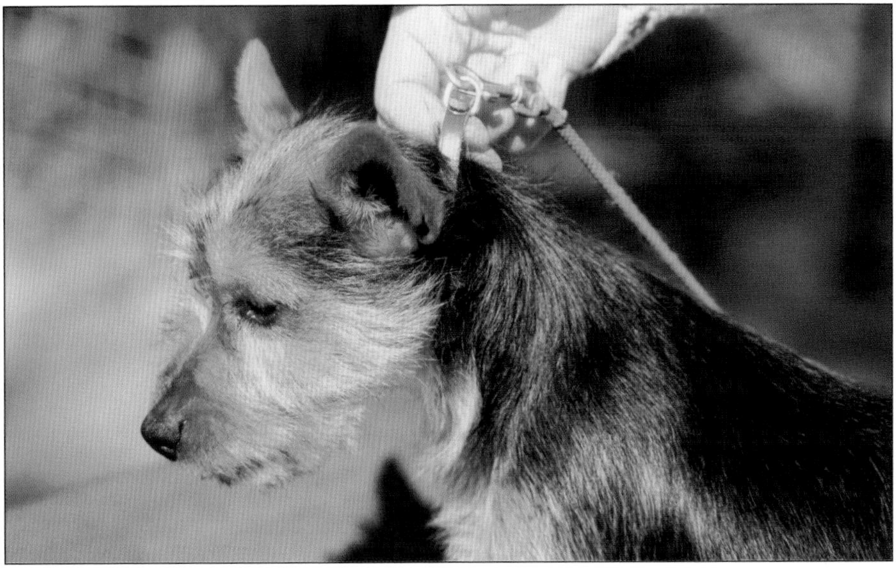

The Australian Terrier puppy should be trained while wearing his everyday collar and a lightweight lead that is easy for you to handle.

GETTING READY FOR SCHOOL

Collar and Leash

Before you begin your Australian Terrier puppy's education, he must be used to his collar and leash. Choose a collar for your puppy that is secure, but not heavy or bulky. He won't enjoy training if he's uncomfortable. A flat buckle collar is fine for everyday wear and for initial puppy training. For older dogs, there are several types of training collars such as the martingale, which is a double loop that tightens slightly around the neck, or the head collar, which is similar to a horse's halter. Do not use a choke collar with your Aussie. Some breeders feel that choke collars are unsuitable for any terrier. The head collar is a much better option for a training collar.

A lightweight 6-foot woven cotton or nylon training leash is preferred by most trainers because it is easy to fold up in your hand and comfortable to hold because there is a certain amount of give to it. There are lessons where the dog will start off 6 feet away from you at the end of the leash. The leash used to take the puppy outside to relieve himself is shorter because you don't want him to roam away from his area. The shorter leash will also be the one to use when you walk the puppy.

If you've been wise enough to enroll in a Puppy Kindergarten training class, suggestions will be made as to the best collar and

BE UPSTANDING!
You are the dog's leader. During training, stand up straight so your dog looks up at you, and therefore up *to* you. Say the command words distinctly, in a clear, declarative tone of voice. (No barking!) Give rewards only as the correct response takes place (remember your timing!). Praise, smiles and treats are "rewards" used to positively reinforce correct responses. Don't repeat a mistake. Just change to another exercise—you will soon find success!

leash for your young puppy. I say "wise" because your puppy will be in a class with puppies in his age range (up to five months old) of all breeds and sizes. It's the perfect way for him to learn the right way (and the wrong way) to interact with other dogs as well as their people. You cannot teach your puppy how to interpret another dog's sign language. For a first-time puppy owner, these socialization classes are invaluable. For experienced dog owners, they are a real boon to further training.

Attention

You've been using the dog's name since the minute you collected him from the breeder, so you should be able to get his attention by saying his name—with a big smile and in an excited tone of voice. His response will be the puppy equivalent of "Here I am! What are we going to do?" Your immediate response (if you haven't guessed by now) is "Good dog." Rewarding him at the moment he pays attention to you teaches him the proper way to respond when he hears his name.

TEACHING THE BASIC COMMANDS

The Sit Exercise

There are several ways to teach the puppy to sit. The first one is to catch him whenever he is about to sit and, as his backside nears the floor, say "Sit, good dog!" That's positive reinforcement and, if your timing is sharp, he will learn that what he's doing at that second is connected to your saying "Sit" and that you think he's clever for doing it!

Another method is to start with the puppy on his leash in front of you. Show him a treat in the palm of your right hand. Bring your hand up under his nose and, almost in slow motion, move your hand up and back so his nose goes up in the air and his head tilts back as he follows the treat in your hand. At that point, he will have to either sit or fall over, so as his back legs buckle under, say "Sit, good dog," and then give him the treat and lots of praise. You may have to begin with your hand lightly running up his chest, actually lifting his chin up until he sits. Some (usually older) dogs require gentle pressure on their hindquarters with the left hand, in which case the dog should be on your left side. Puppies generally do not appreciate this physical dominance.

After a few times, you should be able to show the dog a treat in the open palm of your hand, raise your hand waist-high as you say "Sit" and have him sit. You will thereby have taught him two things at the same time. Both the verbal command and the motion of the hand are signals for the sit. Your puppy is watching you almost more than he is listening to you, so what you do is just as important as what you say.

Don't save any of these drills only for training sessions. Use them as much as possible at odd times during a normal day. The

RIGHT CLICK ON YOUR DOG

With three clicks, the dolphin jumps through the hoop. Wouldn't it be nice to have a dog who could obey wordless commands that easily? Clicker training actually was developed by dolphin trainers and today is used on dogs with great success. You can buy a clicker at a pet shop or pet-supply outlet, and then you'll be off and clicking.

You can click your dog into learning new commands, shaping or conditioning his behavior and solving bad habits. The clicker, used in conjunction with a treat, is an extension of positive reinforcement. The dog begins to recognize your happy clicking, and this becomes a reward in itself. The dog is conditioned to follow your hand with the clicker, just as he would follow your hand with a treat. To discourage the dog from inappropriate behavior (like jumping up or barking), you can use the clicker to set a timeframe and then click and reward the dog once he's waited the allotted time without jumping up or barking.

DOWN

"Down" is a harsh-sounding word and a submissive posture in dog body language, thus presenting two obstacles in teaching the down command. When the dog is about to flop down on his own, tell him "Good down." Pups that are not good about being handled learn better by having food lowered in front of them. A dog that trusts you can be gently guided into position. When you give the command "Down," be sure to say it sweetly!

dog should always sit before being given his food dish. He should sit to let you go through a doorway first, when the doorbell rings or when you stop to speak to someone on the street.

The Down Exercise

Before beginning to teach the down command, you must consider how the dog feels about this exercise. To him, "down" is a submissive position. Being flat on the floor with you standing over him is not his idea of fun. It's up to you to let him know that, while it may not be fun, the reward of your approval is worth his effort.

Start with the puppy on your left side in a sit position. Hold the leash right above his collar in your left hand. Have an extra-special treat, such as a small piece of cooked chicken or hot dog, in your right hand. Place it at the end of the pup's nose and steadily move your hand down and forward along the ground. Hold the leash to prevent a sudden lunge for the food. As the puppy goes into the down position, say "Down" very gently.

The difficulty with this exercise is twofold: it's both the submissive aspect and the fact that most people say the word "Down" as if they were a drill sergeant in charge of recruits! So issue the command sweetly, give him the treat and have the pup maintain the down position for several seconds. If he tries to get up immediately, place your hands on his shoulders and press down gently, giving him a very quiet "Good dog." As you progress with this lesson, increase the "down time" until he will hold it until you say "Okay" (his cue for release). Practice this one in the house at various times throughout the day.

By increasing the length of time during which the dog must maintain the down position, you'll find many uses for it. For example, he can lie at your feet in the vet's office or anywhere that both of you have to wait, when you are on the phone, while the family is eating and so forth. If you progress to training for competitive obedience, he'll already be all set for the exercise called the "long down."

TIME TO PLAY!

Playtime can happen both indoors and out. A young puppy is growing so rapidly that he needs sleep more than he needs a lot of physical exercise. Puppies get sufficient exercise on their own just through normal puppy activity. Monitor play with young children so you can remove the puppy when he's had enough, or calm the kids if they get too rowdy. Almost all puppies love to chase after a toy you've thrown, and you can turn your games into educational activities. Every time your puppy brings the toy back to you, say "Give it" (or "Drop it") followed by "Good dog" and throwing it again. If he's reluctant to give it to you, offer a small treat so that he drops the toy as he takes the treat. He will soon get the idea.

The Stay Exercise

You can teach your Australian Terrier to stay in the sit, down and stand positions. To teach the sit/stay, have the dog sit on your left side. Hold the leash at waist level in your left hand and let the dog know that you have a treat in your closed right hand. Step forward on your right foot as you say "Stay." Immediately turn and stand directly in front of the dog, keeping your right hand up high so he'll keep his eye on the treat hand and maintain the sit position for a count of five. Return to your original position and offer the reward.

Increase the length of the sit/stay each time until the dog can hold it for at least 30 seconds without moving. After about a week of success, move out on your right foot and take two steps before turning to face the dog. Give the "Stay" hand signal (left palm back toward the dog's head) as you leave. He gets the treat when you return and he holds the sit/stay. Increase the distance that you walk away from him before turning until you reach the length of your training leash. But don't rush it! Go back to the beginning if he moves before he should. No matter what the lesson, never be upset by having to back up for a few days. The repetition and practice are what will make your dog reliable in these commands. It won't do any good to move on to something more difficult if the command is not mastered at the easier levels. Above all, even if you do get frustrated, never let your puppy know! Always keep a positive, upbeat attitude during training, which will transmit to your dog for positive results.

The down/stay is taught in the same way once the dog is completely reliable and steady with the down command. Again, don't rush it. With the dog in the down position on your left side, step out on your right foot as you say "Stay." Return by walking around in back of the dog and into your original position. While you are training, it's okay to murmur something like "Hold on" to encourage him to stay put. When the dog will stay without moving when you are at a distance of 3 or 4 feet, begin to increase the length of time before you return. Be sure he holds the down on your return until you say "Okay." At that point, he gets his treat—just so he'll remember for next time that it's not over until it's over.

TIPS FOR TRAINING AND SAFETY

1. Whether on- or off-leash, practice only in a fenced area.
2. Remove the training collar when the training session is over.
3. Don't try to break up a dog fight.
4. "Come," "Leave it" and "Wait" are safety commands.
5. The dog belongs in a crate or behind a barrier when riding in the car.
6. Don't ignore the dog's first sign of aggression. Aggression only gets worse, so take it seriously.
7. Keep the faces of children and dogs separated.
8. Pay attention to what the dog is chewing.
9. Keep the vet's number near your phone.
10. "Okay" is a useful release command.

The Come Exercise

No command is more important to the safety of your Australian Terrier than "Come." It is what you should say every single time you see the puppy running toward you: "Binky, come! Good dog." During playtime, run a few feet away from the puppy and turn and tell him to "Come" as he is already running to you. You can go so far as to teach your puppy two things at once if you squat down and hold out your arms. As the pup gets close to you and you're saying "Good dog," bring your right arm in about waist high. Now he's also learning the hand signal, an excellent device should you be on the phone when you need to get him to come to you! You'll also both be one step ahead when you enter obedience classes.

Encouraging your pup to come to you in the course of playing with him is a precursor to teaching the "Come" command.

When the puppy responds to your well-timed "Come," try it with the puppy on the training leash. This time, catch him off guard, while he's sniffing a leaf or watching a bird: "Binky, come!" You may have to pause for a split second after his name to be sure you have his attention. If the puppy shows any sign of confusion, give the leash a mild jerk and take a couple of steps backward. Do not repeat the command. In this case, you should say "Good come" as he reaches you.

That's the number-one rule of training. Each command word is given just once. Anything more is nagging. You'll also notice that all commands are one word only.

DON'T STRESS ME OUT

Your dog doesn't have to deal with paying the bills, the daily commute, PTA meetings and the like, but, believe it or not, there's lots of stress in a dog's world. Stress can be caused by the owner's impatient demeanor and his angry or harsh corrections. If your dog cringes when you reach for his training collar, he's stressed. An older dog is sometimes stressed out when he goes to a new home. No matter what the cause, put off all training until he's over it. If he's going through a fear period—shying away from people, trembling when spoken to, avoiding eye contact or hiding under furniture—wait to resume training. Naturally you'd also postpone your lessons if the dog were sick, and the same goes for you. Show some compassion.

Always make your dog's coming to you a happy experience. Greet him with a favorite toy and some playtime so that he equates coming to you with fun!

Even when they are actually two words, you say them as one.

Never call the dog to come to you—with or without his name—if you are angry or intend to correct him for some misbehavior. When correcting the pup, you go to him. Your dog must always connect "Come" with something pleasant and with your approval; then you can rely on his response.

Puppies, like children, have notoriously short attention spans, so don't overdo it when teaching the "Come" or any other exercise. Keep each lesson short. Break it up with a quick run around the yard or a ball toss, repeat the lesson and quit as soon as the pup gets it right. That way, you will always end with a "Good dog."

Life isn't perfect and neither are puppies. A time will come, often around ten months of age, when he'll become "selectively deaf" or choose to "forget" his name. He may respond by wagging his tail (and even seeming to smile at you) with a look that says "Make me!" Laugh, throw his favorite toy and skip the lesson you had planned. Pups will be pups!

THE HEEL EXERCISE

The second most important command to teach, after the come, is the heel. When you are walking your growing puppy, you need to be in control. Besides, it looks terrible to be pulled and yanked down the street, and it's not much fun either. Your eight- to ten-week-old puppy will probably follow you everywhere, but that's his natural instinct, not your control over the situation. However, any time he does follow you, you can say "Heel" and be ahead of the game, as he will learn to associate this command with the action of following you before you even begin teaching him to heel.

COME AND GET IT!

The come command is your dog's safety signal. Until he is 99% perfect in responding, don't use the come command if you cannot enforce it. Practice on leash with treats or squeakers, or whenever the dog is running to you. Never call him to come to you if he is to be corrected for a misdemeanor. Reward the dog with a treat and happy praise whenever he comes to you.

There is a very precise, almost military, procedure for teaching your dog to heel. As with all other obedience training, begin with the dog on your left side. He will be in a very nice sit and you will have the training leash across your chest. Hold the loop and folded leash in your right hand. Pick up the slack leash above the dog in your left hand and hold it loosely at your side. Step out on your left foot as you say "Heel." If the puppy does not move, give a gentle tug or pat your left leg to get him started. If he surges ahead of you, stop and pull him back gently until he is at your side. Tell him to sit and begin again.

Walk a few steps and stop while the puppy is correctly beside you. Tell him to sit and give mild verbal praise. (More enthusiastic praise will encourage him to think the lesson is over.) Repeat the lesson, increasing the number of steps you take only as long as the dog is heeling nicely beside you. When you end the lesson, have him hold the sit, then give him the "Okay" to let him know that this is the end of the lesson. Praise him so that he knows he did a good job.

The cure for excessive pulling (a common problem) is to stop when the dog is no more than 2 or 3 feet ahead of you. Guide him back into position and begin again. With a really determined puller, try switching to a head collar. This will automatically turn the pup's head toward you so you can bring him back easily to the heel position. Give quiet, reassuring praise every time the leash goes slack and he's staying with you.

Staying and heeling can take a lot out of a dog, so provide playtime and free-running exercise to shake off the stress when the lessons are over. You don't want him to associate training with all work and no fun.

TAPERING OFF TIDBITS

Your dog has been watching you—and the hand that treats—throughout all of his lessons, and now it's time to break the treat habit. Begin by giving him treats at the end of each lesson only. Then start to give a treat after the end of only some of the lessons. At the end of every lesson, as well as during the lessons, be consistent with the praise. Your pup now doesn't know

OKAY!

This is the signal that tells your dog that he can quit whatever he was doing. Use "Okay" to end a session on a correct response to a command. (Never end on an incorrect response.) Lots of praise follows. People use "Okay" a lot and it has other uses for dogs, too. Your dog is barking. You say, "Okay! Come!" "Okay" signals him to stop the barking activity and "Come" allows him to come to you for a "Good dog."

Count balance and poise among the Australian Terrier's talents.

whether he'll get a treat or not, but he should keep performing well just in case! Finally, you will stop giving treat rewards entirely. Save them for something brand-new that you want to teach him. Keep up the praise and you'll always have a "good dog."

OBEDIENCE CLASSES

The advantages of an obedience class are that your dog will have to learn amid the distractions of other people and dogs and that your mistakes will be quickly corrected by the trainer. Teaching your dog along with a qualified instructor and other handlers who may have more dog experience than you is another plus of the class environment. The instructor and other handlers can help you to find the most efficient way of teaching your dog a command or exercise. It's often easier to learn by other people's mistakes than your own. You will also learn all of the requirements for competitive obedience trials, in which you can earn titles and go on to advanced jumping and retrieving exercises, which are fun for many dogs. Obedience classes build the foundation needed for many other canine activities (in which we humans are allowed to participate, too!).

TRAINING FOR OTHER ACTIVITIES

Once your dog has basic obedience under his collar and is 12 months of age, you can enter the world of agility training. Dogs think agility is pure fun, like being turned loose in an amusement park full of obstacles! In addition to agility, there are activities that are tailor-made for every type of dog. For example, there are hunting activities for sporting dogs, lure-coursing events for sighthounds, go-to-ground events for terriers, racing for the Nordic sled dogs, herding trials for the shepherd breeds and tracking, which is open to all "nosey" dogs (which would include all dogs!).

Aussies can excel in both obedience and agility because of their high energy levels and intelligence, and also because they like to please—unlike some terriers. Earthdog trials are also excellent competitive activities for Aussies, and for all small terriers, because they enjoy the opportunity to use their instinctive going-to-ground abilities.

Dog activities are not limited to just competitive events. For those who like to volunteer, there is the wonderful feeling of owning a Therapy Dog and visiting hospices, nursing homes and veterans' homes to bring smiles, comfort and companionship to those who live there.

Around the house, your Australian Terrier can be taught to do some simple chores. You might teach him to carry a small basket or to fetch certain objects. The kids can teach the dog all kinds of tricks, from playing hide-and-seek to balancing a biscuit on his nose. A family dog is what rounds out the family. Everything he does beyond sitting in your lap or gazing lovingly at you represents the bonus of owning a dog.

GET TO WORK!

The American Working Terrier Association, founded in 1971, is to encourage and preserve the natural instinct of earthdogs. Tests are held in which the dogs are to enter an underground tunnel and to react in a positive manner when facing the quarry. A Working Certificate is issued to dogs who qualify for working in a natural den. The AWTA issues Working, Hunting and Gameness Certificates.

Australian Terriers are amazingly trainable and athletic. Many breed members excel in agility trials, as this high-flying Aussie demonstrates.

Physical Structure of the Australian Terrier

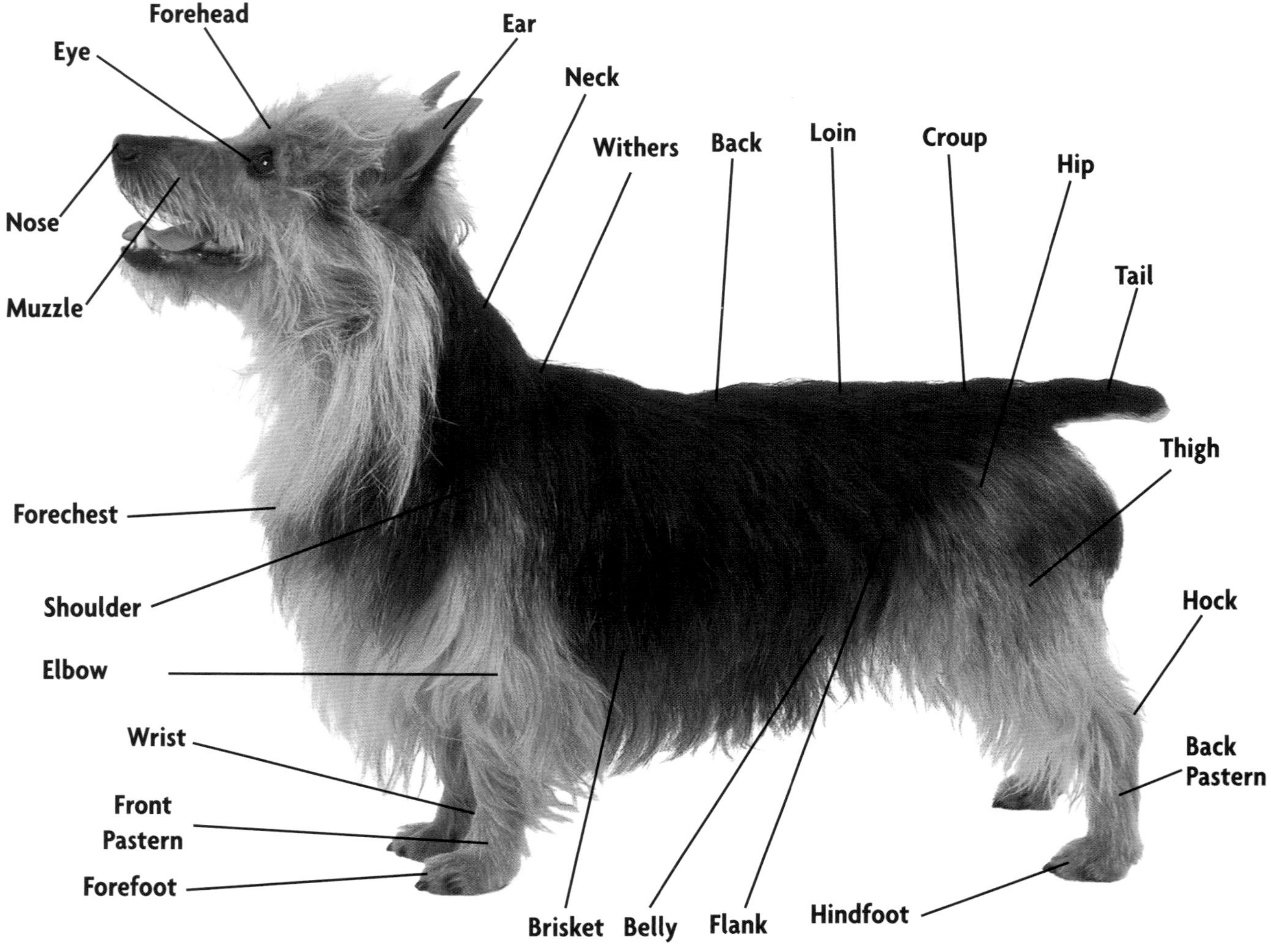

HEALTHCARE OF YOUR
AUSTRALIAN TERRIER

BY LOWELL ACKERMAN DVM, DACVD

HEALTHCARE FOR A LIFETIME

When you own a dog, you become his healthcare advocate over his entire lifespan, as well as being the one to shoulder the financial burden of such care. Accordingly, it is worthwhile to focus on prevention rather than treatment, as you and your pet will both be happier.

Of course, the best place to have begun your program of preventive healthcare is with the initial purchase or adoption of your dog. There is no way of guaranteeing that your new furry friend is free of medical problems, but there are some things you can do to improve your odds. You certainly should have done adequate research into the Australian Terrier and have selected your puppy carefully rather than buying on impulse. Health issues aside, a large number of pet abandonment and relinquishment cases arise from a mismatch between pet needs and owner expectations. This is entirely preventable with appropriate planning and finding a good breeder.

Regarding healthcare issues specifically, it is very difficult to make blanket statements about where to acquire a problem-free pet, but, again, a reputable breeder is your best bet. In an ideal situation, you have the opportunity to see both parents, get references from other owners of the breeder's pups and see genetic-testing documentation for several generations of the litter's ancestors. At the very least, you must thoroughly investigate your breed of interest and the problems inherent in that breed, as well as the genetic testing available to screen for those problems. Genetic testing offers some important benefits, but testing is available for only a few disorders in a relatively small number of breeds and is not available for some of the most common genetic diseases, such as hip dysplasia, cataracts, epilepsy, cardiomyopathy, etc. This area of research is indeed exciting and increasingly important, and advances will continue to be made each year. In fact, recent research has shown that

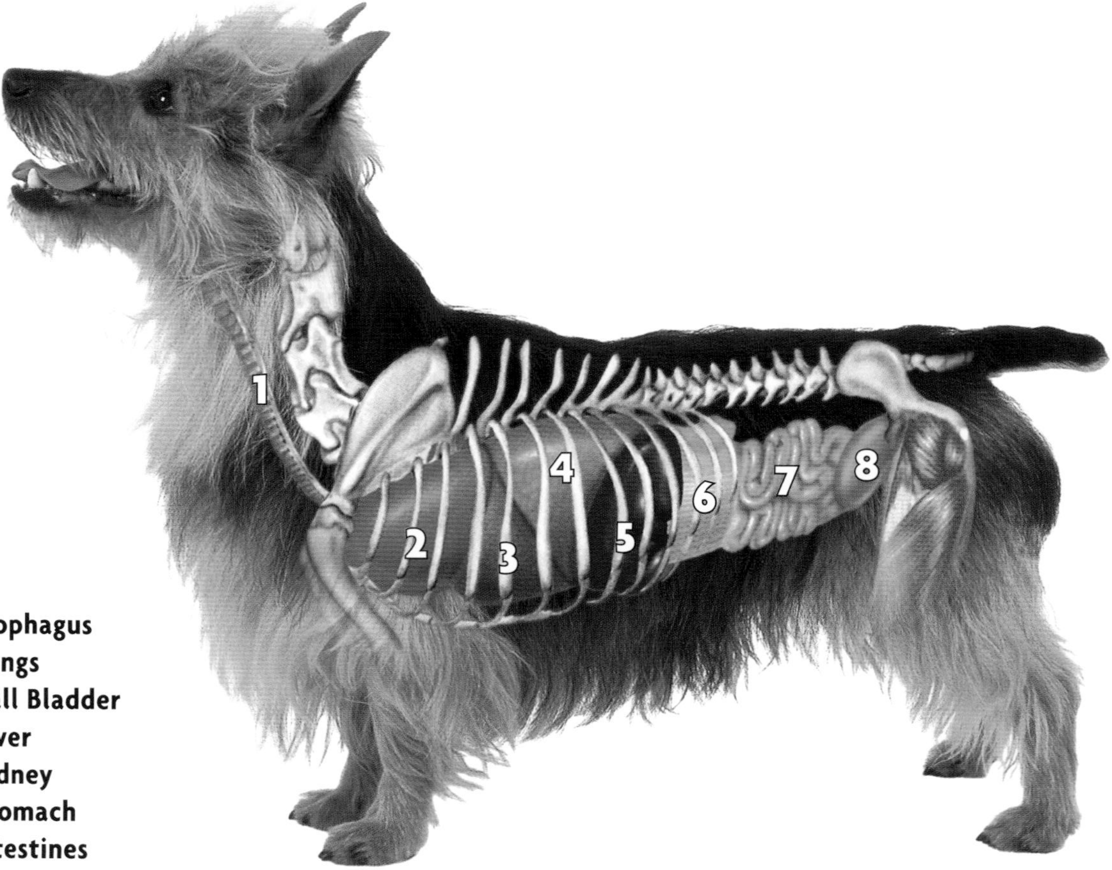

1. Esophagus
2. Lungs
3. Gall Bladder
4. Liver
5. Kidney
6. Stomach
7. Intestines
8. Urinary Bladder

there is an equivalent dog gene for 75% of known human genes, so research done in either species is likely to benefit the other.

We've also discussed that evaluating the behavioral nature of your Australian Terrier and that of his immediate family members is an important part of the selection process that cannot be underestimated or overemphasized. It is sometimes difficult to evaluate temperament in puppies because certain behavioral tendencies, such as some forms of aggression, may not be immediately evident. More dogs are euthanized each year for behavioral reasons than for all medical conditions combined, so it is critical to take temperament issues seriously. Start with a well-balanced, friendly companion and put the time and effort into proper socialization, and you will both be rewarded with a lifelong valued relationship.

Assuming that you have started off with a pup from healthy, sound stock, you then become responsible for helping your veterinarian keep your pet healthy. Some crucial things happen before you even bring your puppy home. Parasite control typically begins at two weeks of age, and vaccinations typically begin at six to eight weeks of age. A pre-pubertal evaluation is typically scheduled for about six months of age. At this time, a dental evaluation is done (since the adult teeth are now in), heartworm prevention is started and neutering or spaying is most commonly done.

It is critical to commence regular dental care at home if you have not already done so. It may not sound very important, but most dogs have active periodontal disease by four years of age if they don't have their teeth cleaned regularly at home, not just at their veterinary exams. Dental problems lead to more than just bad "doggie breath": gum disease can have very serious medical consequences. If you start brushing your dog's teeth and using antiseptic rinses from a young age, your dog will be accustomed to it and will not resist. The results will be healthy dentition, which your pet will need to enjoy a long, healthy life.

DOGGIE DENTAL DON'TS

A veterinary dental exam is necessary if you notice one or any combination of the following in your dog:

- Broken, loose or missing teeth
- Loss of appetite (which could be due to mouth pain or illness caused by infection)
- Gum abnormalities, including redness, swelling and bleeding
- Drooling, with or without blood
- Yellowing of the teeth or gumline, indicating tartar
- Bad breath

Skeletal Structure of the Australian Terrier

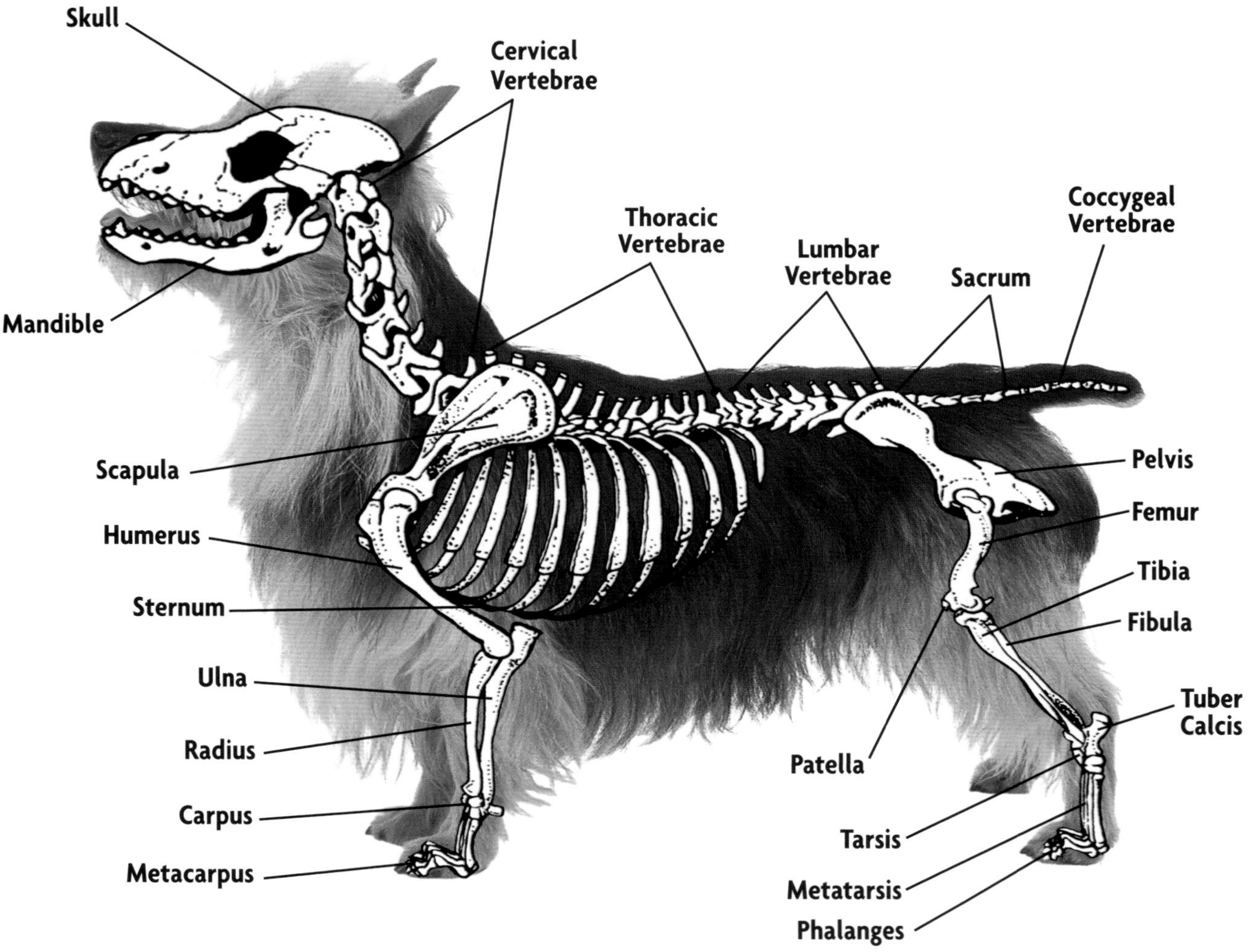

Most dogs are considered adults at a year of age, although some larger breeds still have some filling out to do up to about two or so years old. Even individual dogs within each breed have different healthcare requirements, so work with your veterinarian to determine what will be needed and what your role should be. This doctor-client relationship is important, because as vaccination guidelines change, there may not be an annual "vaccine visit" scheduled. You must make sure that you see your veterinarian at least annually, even if no vaccines are due, because this is the best opportunity to coordinate healthcare activities and to make sure that no medical issues creep by unaddressed.

When your Australian Terrier reaches three-quarters of his anticipated lifespan, he is considered a "senior" and likely requires some special care. In general, if you've been taking great care of your canine companion throughout his formative and adult years, the transition to senior status should be a smooth one. Age is not a disease, and as long as everything is functioning as it should, there is no reason why most of late adulthood should not be rewarding for both you and your pet. This is especially true if you have tended to the details, such as regular veterinary visits, proper dental care, excellent nutrition and management of bone and joint issues.

YOUR DOG NEEDS TO VISIT THE VET IF:

- He has ingested a toxin such as antifreeze or a toxic plant; in these cases, administer first aid and call the vet right away
- His teeth are discolored, loose or missing or he has sores or other signs of infection or abnormality in the mouth
- He has been vomiting, has had diarrhea or has been constipated for over 24 hours; call immediately if you notice blood
- He has refused food for over 24 hours
- His eating habits, water intake or toilet habits have noticeably changed; if you have noticed weight gain or weight loss
- He shows symptoms of bloat, which requires immediate attention
- He is salivating excessively
- He has a lump in his throat
- He has a lumps or bumps anywhere on the body
- He is very lethargic
- He appears to be in pain or otherwise has trouble chewing or swallowing
- His skin loses elasticity

Of course, there will be other instances in which a visit to the vet is necessary; these are just some of the signs that could be indicative of serious problems that need to be caught as early as possible.

At this stage in your Australian Terrier's life, your veterinarian may want to schedule visits twice yearly, instead of once, to run some laboratory screenings, electrocardiograms and the like, and to change the diet to something more digestible. Catching problems early is the best way to manage them effectively. Treating the early stages of heart disease is so much easier than trying to intervene when there is more significant damage to the heart muscle. Similarly, managing the beginning of kidney problems is fairly routine if there is no significant kidney damage. Other problems, like cognitive dysfunction (similar to senility and Alzheimer's disease), cancer, diabetes and arthritis, are more common in older dogs, but all can be treated to help the dog live as many happy, comfortable years as possible. Just as in people, medical management is more effective (and less expensive) when you catch things early.

PROBLEM: AND THAT STARTS WITH "P"

Urinary tract problems more commonly affect female dogs, especially those who have been spayed. The first sign that a urinary tract problem exists usually is a strong odor from the urine or an unusual color. Blood in the urine, known as hematuria, is another sign of an infection, related to cystitis, a bladder infection, bladder cancer or a blood-clotting disorder. Urinary tract problems can also be signaled by the dog's straining while urinating, experiencing pain during urination and genital discharge as well as excessive water intake and urination.

Excessive drinking, in and of itself, does not indicate a urinary tract problem. A dog who is drinking more than normal may have a kidney or liver problem, a hormonal disorder or diabetes mellitus. Behaviorists report a disorder known as psychogenic polydipsia, which manifests itself in excessive drinking and urination. If you notice your dog drinking much more than normal, take him to the vet.

SELECTING A VETERINARIAN

There is probably no more important decision that you will make regarding your pet's healthcare than the selection of his doctor. Your pet's veterinarian will be a pediatrician, family-practice physician and gerontologist, depending on the dog's life stage, and will be the individual who makes recommendations regarding issues such as when specialists need to be consulted, when diagnostic testing and/or therapeutic intervention is needed and when you will need to seek outside emergency and critical-care services. Your vet will act as your advocate and liaison throughout these processes.

Everyone has his own idea about what to look for in a vet, an individual who will play a big role in his dog's (and, of course, his own) life for many years to come. For some, it is the compassionate caregiver with whom they hope to develop a professional relationship to span the lifetime of their dogs and even their future pets. For others, they are seeking a clinician with keen diagnostic and therapeutic insight who can deliver state-of-the-art healthcare. Still others need a veterinary facility that is open evenings and weekends, or is in close proximity or provides mobile veterinary services, to accommodate their schedules; these people may not much mind that their dogs might see different veterinarians on each visit. Just as we have different reasons for selecting our own healthcare professionals (e.g., covered by insurance plan, expert in field, convenient location, etc.), we should not expect that there is a one-size-fits-all recommendation for selecting a veterinarian and veterinary practice. The best advice is to be honest in your assessment of what you expect from a veterinary practice and to conscientiously research the options in your area. You will quickly appreciate that not all veterinary practices are the same, and you will be happiest with one that truly meets your needs.

There is another point to be considered in the selection of veterinary services. Not that long ago, a single veterinarian would attempt to manage all medical and surgical issues as they arose. That was often problematic, because veterinarians are trained in many species and many diseases, and it was just impossible for general veterinary practitioners to be experts in every species, every field and every ailment. However, just as in the human healthcare fields, specialization has allowed general practitioners to concentrate on primary healthcare delivery, especially wellness and the prevention of infectious diseases, and to utilize a network of specialists to assist in the management of conditions that require specific expertise and experience. Thus there are now many types of veterinary specialists, including dermatologists, cardiologists, ophthalmologists, surgeons, internists, oncologists, neurologists, behaviorists, criticalists and others to help primary-care veterinarians deal with complicated medical challenges. In most cases, specialists see cases referred by primary-care veterinarians, make diagnoses and set up management plans. From there, the animals' ongoing care is returned to their primary-care veterinarians. This important team approach to your pet's medical-care needs has provided opportunities for

TAKING YOUR DOG'S TEMPERATURE

It is important to know how to take your dog's temperature at times when you think he may be ill. It's not the most enjoyable task, but it can be done without too much difficulty. It's easier with a helper, preferably someone with whom the dog is friendly, so that one of you can hold the dog while the other inserts the thermometer.

Before inserting the thermometer, coat the end with petroleum jelly. Insert the thermometer slowly and gently into the dog's rectum about one inch. Wait for the reading, about two minutes. Be sure to remove the thermometer carefully and clean it thoroughly after each use.

A dog's normal body temperature is between 100.5 and 102.5 degrees F. Immediate veterinary attention is required if the dog's temperature is below 99 or above 104 degrees F.

advanced care and an unparalleled level of quality to be delivered.

With all of the opportunities for your Australian Terrier to receive high-quality veterinary medical care, there is another topic that needs to be addressed at the same time—cost. It's been said that you can have excellent healthcare or inexpensive healthcare, but never both; this is as true in veterinary medicine as it is in human medicine. While veterinary costs are a fraction of what the same services cost in the human healthcare arena, it is still difficult to deal with unanticipated medical costs, especially since they can easily creep into hundreds or even thousands of dollars if specialists or emergency services become involved. However, there are ways of managing these risks. The easiest is to buy pet health insurance and realize that its foremost purpose is not to cover routine healthcare visits but rather to serve as an umbrella for those rainy days when your pet needs medical care and you don't want to worry about whether or not you can afford that care.

Pet insurance policies are very cost-effective (and very inexpensive by human health-insurance standards), but make sure that you buy the policy long before you intend to use it (preferably starting in puppyhood, because coverage will exclude pre-existing conditions) and that you are actually buying an indemnity insurance plan from an insurance company that is regulated by your state or province. Many insurance policy look-alikes are actually discount clubs that are redeemable only at specific locations and for specific services. An indemnity plan covers your pet at almost all veterinary, specialty and emergency practices and is an excellent way to manage your pet's ongoing healthcare needs.

VACCINATIONS AND INFECTIOUS DISEASES

There has never been an easier time to prevent a variety of infectious diseases in your dog, but the advances we've made in veterinary medicine come with a price—choice. Now while it may seem that choice is a good thing (and it is), it has never been more difficult for the pet owner (or the veterinarian) to make an informed decision about the best way to protect pets through vaccination.

Years ago, it was just accepted that puppies got a starter series of vaccinations and then annual "boosters" throughout their lives to keep them protected. As more and more vaccines became available, consumers wanted the convenience of having all of that protection in a single injection. The result was "multivalent" vaccines that crammed a lot of protection into a single syringe. The manufacturers' recommendations were to give the vaccines annually, and this was a simple enough protocol to follow. However, as veterinary medicine has become more sophisticated and we have started looking more at healthcare quandaries rather than convenience, it became necessary to reevaluate the situation and deal with some tough questions.

It is important to realize that whether or not to use a particular vaccine depends on the risk of contracting the disease against which it protects, the severity of the disease if it is contracted, the duration of immunity provided by the vaccine, the safety of the product and the needs of the individual animal. In a very general sense, rabies, distemper, hepatitis and parvovirus are considered core vaccine needs, while parainfluenza, *Bordetella bronchiseptica*, leptospirosis, coronavirus and borreliosis (Lyme disease) are considered non-core needs and best reserved for animals that demonstrate reasonable risk of contracting the diseases.

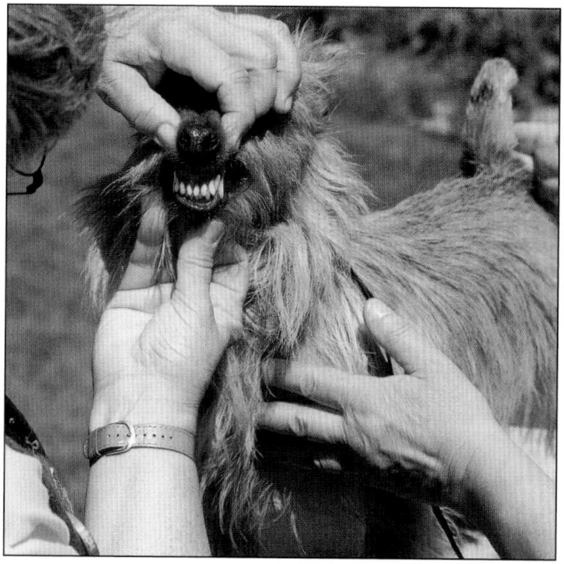

Whether show dog or pet, every Australian Terrier should have complete dentition and clean, healthy teeth and gums.

THE GREAT VACCINATION DEBATE

What kinds of questions need to be addressed? When the vet

injects multiple organisms at the same time, might some of the components interfere with one another in the development of immunologic protection? We don't have the comprehensive answer for that question, but it does appear that the immune system better handles agents when given individually. Unfortunately, most manufacturers still bundle their vaccine components because that is what most pet owners want, so getting vaccines with single components can sometimes be difficult.

Another question has to do with how often vaccines should be given. Again, this seems to be different for each vaccine component. There seems to be a general consensus that a puppy (or a dog with an unknown vaccination history) should get a series of vaccinations to initially stimulate his immunity and then a booster at one year of age, but even the veterinary associations and colleges have trouble reaching agreement about what he should get after that. Rabies vaccination schedules are not debated, because vaccine schedules for this contagious and devastating disease are determined by government agencies. Regarding the rest, some recommend that we

Sample Vaccination Schedule

6–8 weeks of age	Parvovirus, Distemper, Adenovirus-2 (Hepatitis)
9–11 weeks of age	Parvovirus, Distemper, Adenovirus-2 (Hepatitis)
12–14 weeks of age	Parvovirus, Distemper, Adenovirus-2 (Hepatitis)
16–20 weeks of age	Rabies
1 year of age	Parvovirus, Distemper, Adenovirus-2 (Hepatitis), Rabies

Revaccination is performed every one to three years, depending on the product, the method of administration and the patient's risk. Initial adult inoculation (for dogs at least 16 weeks of age in which a puppy series was not done or could not be confirmed) is two vaccinations, done three to four weeks apart, with revaccination according to the same criteria mentioned. Other vaccines are given as decided between owner and veterinarian.

continue to give the vaccines annually because this method has worked well as a disease preventive for decades and delivers predictable protection. Others recommend that some of the vaccines need to be given only every second or third year, as this can be done without affecting levels of protection. This is probably true for some vaccine components (such as hepatitis), but there have been no large studies to demonstrate what the optimal interval should be and whether the same principles hold true for all breeds.

After your Aussie has been playing in the yard, examine his coat for parasites, such as ticks and fleas, and any debris that he may have picked up in his coat.

BEWARE THE SPIDER

Should you worry about having a spider spinning her mucilaginous web over your dog? Like other venomous critters, spiders can bite dogs and cause severe reactions. The most deleterious eight-leggers are the black and red widow spiders, brown recluse and common brown spiders, whose bites can cause local pain, cramping, spasms and restlessness. These signals tell owners there is a problem, as the bites themselves can be difficult to locate under your dog's coat. Another vicious arachnid is the bark scorpion, whose bite can cause excessive drooling, tearing, urination and defecation. Often spider and scorpion bites are misdiagnosed because vets don't recognize the signs and owners didn't witness the escape of the avenging arachnid.

It may be best to just measure titers, which are protective blood levels of various vaccine components, on an annual basis, but that too is not without controversy. Scientists have not precisely determined the minimum titer of specific vaccine components that will be guaranteed to provide a pet with protection. Pets with very high titers will clearly be protected and those with very low titers will need repeat vaccinations, but there is also a large "gray zone" of pets that probably have intermediate protection and may or may not need repeat vaccination, depending on their risk of coming into contact with the disease.

These questions leave primary-care veterinarians in a very uncomfortable position, one

Allergies often can be traced to a dog's diet; in these cases, changes to the diet can work wonders in alleviating the dog's symptoms.

that is not easy to resolve. Do they recommend annual vaccination in a manner that has demonstrated successful protection for decades, do they recommend skipping vaccines some years and hope that the protection lasts or do they measure blood tests (titers) and hope that the results are convincing enough to clearly indicate whether repeat vaccination is warranted?

These aren't the only vaccination questions impacting pets, owners and veterinarians. Other controversies focus on whether vaccines should be dosed according to body weight (currently they are administered in uniform doses, regardless of the animal's size), whether there are breed-specific issues important in determining vaccination programs (for instance, we know that some breeds have a harder time mounting an appropriate immune response to parvovirus vaccine and might benefit from a different dose or injection interval) and which type of vaccine—live-virus or inactivated—offers more advantages with fewer disadvantages. Clearly, there are many more questions than there are answers. The important thing, as a pet owner, is to be aware of the issues and be able to work with your veterinarian to make decisions that are right for your pet. Be an informed consumer and you will appreciate the deliberation required in tailoring a vaccination program to best meet the needs of your pet. Expect also that this is an ongoing, ever-changing topic of debate; thus, the decisions you make this year won't necessarily be the same as the ones you make next year.

Common Vaccinations

Now that you are more confused than ever about vaccination, it is a

What's itching your Aussie? All dogs enjoy a good scratch, but excessive scratching usually indicates a more serious problem.

Proper diet, training, exercise and attentive care will result in a wonderful Australian Terrier pet who will be with you for many years.

good time to discuss some of the diseases that create the need for vaccination in the first place. Following are the major canine infectious diseases and a simple explanation of each.

Rabies is a devastating viral disease that can be fatal in dogs and people. In fact, vaccination of dogs and cats is an important public-health measure to create a resistant animal buffer population to protect people from contracting the disease. Vaccination schedules are determined on a government level and are not optional for pet owners; rabies vaccination is required by law in all 50 states.

Parvovirus is a severe, potentially life-threatening disease that is easily transmitted between dogs. There are four strains of the virus, but it is believed that there is significant "cross-protection" between strains that may be included in individual vaccines.

Distemper is another potentially severe and life-threatening disease with a relatively high risk of exposure, especially in certain regions. In very high-risk distemper environments, young pups may be vaccinated with human measles vaccine, a related virus that offers cross-protection when administered at 4–10 weeks of age.

Hepatitis is caused by canine adenovirus type 1 (CAV-1), but since vaccination with the causative virus has a higher rate of adverse effects, cross-protection is derived from the use of adenovirus type 2 (CAV-2), a cause of respiratory disease and one of the potential causes of canine cough. Vaccination with CAV-2 provides long-term immunity against hepatitis, but relatively less protection against respiratory infection.

Canine cough (tracheobronchitis) is actually a fairly complicated result of viral and bacterial offenders; therefore, even with vaccination, protection is incomplete. Wherever dogs congregate, canine cough will likely be spread among them. Intranasal vaccination with *Bordetella* and parainfluenza is the best safeguard, but the duration of immunity does not appear to be very long, typically a year at most. These are non-core vaccines, but vaccination is sometimes mandated by boarding kennels, obedience classes, dog shows and other places where dogs congregate to try to minimize spread of infection.

Leptospirosis is a potentially fatal disease that is more common in some geographic regions. It is capable of being spread to humans. The disease varies with the individual "serovar," or strain, of *Leptospira* involved; since there does not appear to be much cross-protection between serovars, protection is only as good as the likelihood that the serovar in the vaccine is the same as the one in the pet's local environment. Problems with *Leptospira* vaccines are that protection does not last very long, side effects are not uncommon and a large percentage of dogs (perhaps 30%) may not respond to vaccination.

Lyme disease is caused by *Borrelia burgdorferi*; the risk of being infected varies with the geographic area in which the pet lives and travels. Lyme disease is spread by deer ticks in the eastern US and western black-legged ticks in the western part of the country, and the risk of exposure is high in some regions. Lameness, fever and inappetence are most commonly seen in affected dogs. The extent of protection from the vaccine has not been conclusively demonstrated.

Coronavirus has a high risk of exposure, especially in areas where dogs congregate, but it typically causes only mild to moderate digestive upset (diarrhea, vomiting, etc.). Vaccines are available, but the duration of protection is believed to be relatively short and the effectiveness of the vaccine in preventing infection is considered low.

There are many other vaccinations available, including those for *Giardia* and canine adenovirus-1. While there may be some specific indications for their use, and local risk factors to be considered, they are not widely recommended for most dogs.

NEUTERING/SPAYING

Sterilization procedures (neutering for males/spaying for females) are meant to accomplish several purposes. While the underlying premise is to address the risk of pet overpopulation, there are also some medical and behavioral benefits to the surgeries as well. For females, spaying prior to the first estrus (heat cycle) leads to a marked reduction in the risk of mammary cancer. There also will be no manifestations of "heat" to attract male dogs and no bleeding in the house. For males, there is prevention of testicular cancer and a reduction in the risk of prostate problems. In both sexes, there may be some limited reduction in aggressive behaviors toward other dogs, and some diminishing of urine marking, roaming and mounting.

While neutering and spaying do indeed prevent animals from contributing to pet overpopulation, even no-cost and low-cost neutering options have not eliminated the problem. Perhaps one of the main reasons for this is that individuals who intentionally breed their dogs and those who allow their animals to run at large are the main causes of unwanted offspring. Also, animals in shelters are often there because they were abandoned or relinquished, not because they came from unplanned matings. Neutering/spaying is important, but it should be considered in the context of the real causes of animals' ending up in shelters and eventually being euthanized.

One of the important considerations regarding neutering is that it is a surgical procedure. This sometimes gets lost in discussions of low-cost procedures and commoditization of the process. In females, spaying is specifically referred to as an ovariohysterectomy. In this procedure, a midline incision is made in the abdomen and the entire uterus and both ovaries are surgically removed. While this is a major invasive surgical procedure, it usually has few complications, because it is typically performed on healthy young animals. However, it is major surgery, as any woman who has had a hysterectomy will attest.

In males, neutering has traditionally referred to castration, which involves the surgical removal of both testicles. While still a significant piece of surgery, there is not the abdominal exposure that is required in the female surgery. In addition, there is now a chemical sterilization option, in which a solution is injected into each testicle, leading to atrophy of the sperm-producing cells. This can typically be done under sedation rather than full anesthesia. This is a relatively new approach, and there are no long-term clinical studies yet available.

Neutering/spaying is typically done around six months of age at most veterinary hospitals, although techniques have been pioneered to perform the procedures in animals as young as eight weeks of age. In general, the surgeries on the very young animals are done for the specific reason of sterilizing them before they go to their new homes. This is done in some shelter hospitals for assurance that the animals will definitely not produce any pups. Otherwise, these organizations need to rely on owners to comply with their wishes to have the animals "altered" at a later date, something that does not always happen.

There are some exciting immunocontraceptive "vaccines" currently under development, and there may be a time when contraception in pets will not require surgical procedures. We anxiously await these developments.

HEARTWORM ZONE

Although heartworm cases have been reported in all 48 continental states, the largest threat exists in the Southeast and Mississippi River Valley. The following states have the highest risk factors: Texas, Florida, Louisiana, North Carolina, Georgia, Mississippi, Tennessee, South Carolina, Alabama and Indiana. Discuss the risk factor with your veterinarian to determine the best course of prevention for your dog.

Number-One Killer Disease in Dogs: CANCER

In every age, there is a word associated with a disease or plague that causes humans to shudder. In the 21st century, that word is "cancer." Just as cancer is the leading cause of death in humans, it claims nearly half the lives of dogs that die from a natural disease as well as half the dogs that die over the age of ten years.

Described as a genetic disease, cancer becomes a greater risk as the dog ages. Vets and dog owners have become increasingly aware of the threat of cancer to dogs. Statistics reveal that one dog in every five will develop cancer, the most common of which is skin cancer. Many cancers, including prostate, ovarian and breast cancer, can be avoided by spaying and neutering our dogs by the age of six months.

Early detection of cancer can save or extend a dog's life, so it is absolutely vital for owners to have their dogs examined by a qualified vet or oncologist immediately upon detection of any abnormality. Certain dietary guidelines have also proven to reduce the onset and spread of cancer. Foods based on fish rather than beef, due to the presence of Omega-3 fatty acids, are recommended. Other amino acids such as glutamine have significant benefits for canines, particularly those breeds that show a greater susceptibility to cancer.

Cancer management and treatments promise hope for future generations of canines. Since the disease is genetic, breeders should never breed a dog whose parents, grandparents and any related siblings have developed cancer. It is difficult to know whether to exclude an otherwise healthy dog from a breeding program, as the disease does not manifest itself until the dog's senior years.

RECOGNIZE CANCER WARNING SIGNS

Since early detection can possibly rescue your dog from becoming a cancer statistic, it is essential for owners to recognize the possible signs and seek the assistance of a qualified professional.

- Abnormal bumps or lumps that continue to grow
- Bleeding or discharge from any body cavity
- Persistent stiffness or lameness
- Recurrent sores or sores that do not heal
- Inappetence
- Breathing difficulties
- Weight loss
- Bad breath or odors
- General malaise and fatigue
- Eating and swallowing problems
- Difficulty urinating and defecating

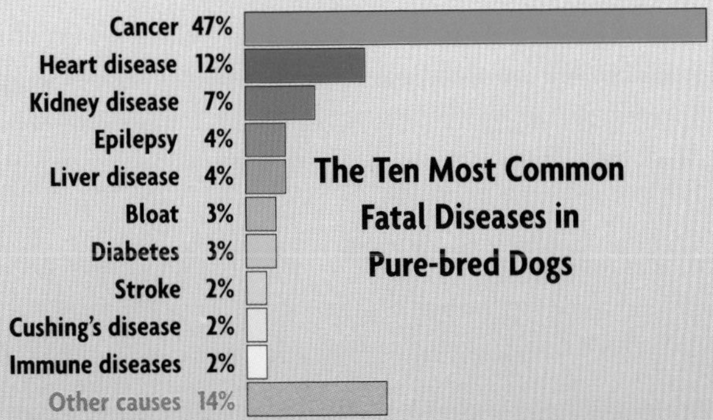

The Ten Most Common Fatal Diseases in Pure-bred Dogs

THE ABCs OF Emergency Care

Abrasions
Clean wound with running water or 3% hydrogen peroxide. Pat dry with gauze and spray with antibiotic. Do not cover.

Animal Bites
Clean area with soap and saline solution or water. Apply pressure to any bleeding area. Apply antibiotic ointment.

Antifreeze Poisoning
Induce vomiting and take dog to the vet.

Bee Sting
Remove stinger and apply soothing lotion or cold compress; give antihistamine in proper dosage.

Bleeding
Apply pressure directly to wound with gauze or towel for five to ten minutes. If wound does not stop bleeding, wrap wound with gauze and adhesive tape.

Bloat/Gastric Torsion
Immediately take the dog to the vet or emergency clinic; phone from car. No time to waste.

Burns
Chemical: Bathe dog with water and pet shampoo. Rinse in saline solution. Apply antibiotic ointment.

Acid: Rinse with water. Apply one part baking soda, two parts water to affected area.

Alkali: Rinse with water. Apply one part vinegar, four parts water to affected area.

Electrical: Apply antibiotic ointment. Seek veterinary assistance immediately.

Choking
If the dog is on the verge of collapsing, wedge a solid object, such as the handle of screwdriver, between molars on one side of mouth to keep mouth open. Pull tongue out. Use long-nosed pliers or fingers to remove foreign object. Do not push the object down the dog's throat. For small or medium dogs, hold dog upside down by hind legs and shake firmly to dislodge foreign object.

Chlorine Ingestion
With clean water, rinse the mouth and eyes. Give dog water to drink; contact the vet.

Constipation
Feed dog 2 tablespoons bran flakes with each meal. Encourage drinking water. Mix $\frac{1}{4}$ teaspoon mineral oil in dog's food.

Diarrhea
Withhold food for 12 to 24 hours. Feed dog anti-diarrheal with eyedropper. When feeding resumes, feed one part boiled hamburger, one part plain cooked rice, $\frac{1}{4}$ to $\frac{3}{4}$ cup four times daily.

Dog Bite
Snip away hair around puncture wound; clean with 3% hydrogen peroxide; apply tincture of iodine. If wound appears deep, take the dog to the vet.

Frostbite
Wrap the dog in a heavy blanket. Warm affected area with a warm bath for ten minutes. Red color to skin will return with circulation; if tissues are pale after 20 minutes, contact the vet.

Use a portable, durable container large enough to contain all items

DOG OWNER'S FIRST-AID KIT

- ❑ Gauze bandages/swabs
- ❑ Adhesive and non-adhesive bandages
- ❑ Antibiotic powder
- ❑ Antiseptic wash
- ❑ Hydrogen peroxide 3%
- ❑ Antibiotic ointment
- ❑ Lubricating jelly
- ❑ Rectal thermometer
- ❑ Nylon muzzle
- ❑ Scissors and forceps
- ❑ Eyedropper
- ❑ Syringe
- ❑ Anti-bacterial/fungal solution
- ❑ Saline solution
- ❑ Antihistamine
- ❑ Cotton balls
- ❑ Nail clippers
- ❑ Screwdriver/pen knife
- ❑ Flashlight
- ❑ Emergency phone numbers

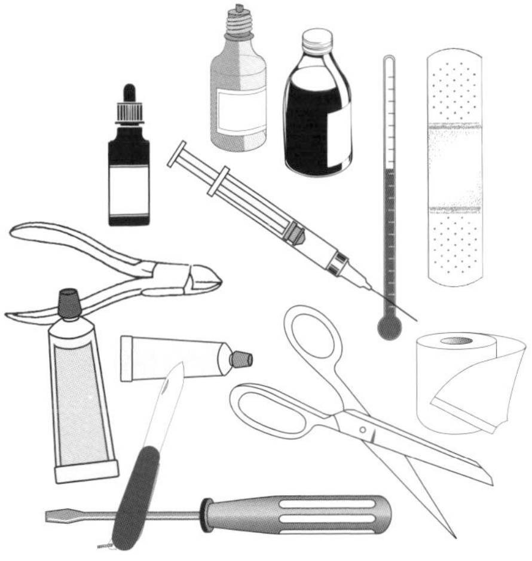

Heat Stroke
Submerge the dog in cold water; if no response within ten minutes, contact the vet.

Hot Spots
Mix 2 packets Domeboro® with 2 cups water. Saturate cloth with mixture and apply to hot spots for 15–30 minutes. Apply antibiotic ointment. Repeat every six to eight hours.

Poisonous Plants
Wash affected area with soap and water. Cleanse with alcohol. For foxtail/grass, apply antibiotic ointment.

Rat Poison Ingestion
Induce vomiting. Keep dog calm, maintain dog's normal body temperature (use blanket or heating pad). Get to the vet for antidote.

Shock
Keep the dog calm and warm; call for veterinary assistance.

Snake Bite
If possible, bandage the area and apply pressure. If the area is not conducive to bandaging, use ice to control bleeding. Get immediate help from the vet.

Tick Removal
Apply flea and tick spray directly on tick. Wait one minute. Using tweezers or wearing plastic gloves, grasp the tick's body firmly. Apply antibiotic ointment.

Vomiting
Restrict dog's water intake; offer a few ice cubes. Withhold food for next meal. Contact vet if vomiting persists longer than 24 hours.

S. E. M. by Dr. Dennis Kunkel, University of Hawaii.

A scanning electron micrograph of a dog flea, *Ctenocephalides canis*, on dog hair

EXTERNAL PARASITES

FLEAS

Fleas have been around for millions of years and, while we have better tools now for controlling them than at any time in the past, there still is little chance that they will end up on an endangered species list. Actually, they are very well adapted to living on our pets, and they continue to adapt as we make advances.

The female flea can consume 15 times her weight in blood during active reproduction and can lay as many as 40 eggs a day. These eggs are very resistant to the effects of insecticides. They hatch into larvae, which then mature and spin cocoons. The immature fleas reside in this pupal stage until the time is right for feeding. This pupal stage is also very resistant to the effects of insecticides, and pupae can last in the environment without feeding for many months. Newly emergent fleas are attracted to animals by the warmth of the animals' bodies, movement and exhaled carbon dioxide. However, when they first emerge from their cocoons, they orient towards light; thus when an animal passes between a flea and the light source, casting a shadow, the flea pounces and starts to feed. If the animal turns out to be a dog or cat, the reproductive cycle continues. If the flea lands on another type of animal, including a person, the flea will bite but will then look for a more appropriate host. An emerging adult flea can survive without feeding for up to 12 months but, once it tastes blood, it can survive off its host for only three to four days.

It was once thought that fleas spend most of their lives in the environment, but we now know that fleas won't willingly jump off a dog unless leaping to another dog or when physically removed by brushing, bathing or other manipulation. Flea eggs, on the other hand, are shiny and smooth, and they roll off the animal and into the environment. The eggs, larvae and pupae then exist in the environment, but once the adult finds a susceptible animal, it's home sweet home until the flea is forced to seek refuge elsewhere.

Since adult fleas live on the animal and immature forms survive in the environment, a successful treatment plan must address all stages of the flea life cycle. There are now several safe and effective flea-control products that can be applied on a monthly basis. These include fipronil, imidacloprid, selamectin and permethrin (found in several formulations). Most of these products have significant flea-killing rates within 24 hours. However, none of them will control the immature forms in the environment. To accomplish this, there are a variety of insect growth regulators that can be sprayed into

FLEA PREVENTION FOR YOUR DOG

- Discuss with your veterinarian the safest product to protect your dog, likely in the form of a monthly tablet or a liquid preparation placed on the back of the dog's neck.
- For dogs suffering from flea-bite dermatitis, a shampoo or topical insecticide treatment is required.
- Your lawn and property should be sprayed with an insecticide designed to kill fleas and ticks that lurk outdoors.
- Using a flea comb, check the dog's coat regularly for any signs of parasites.
- Practice good housekeeping. Vacuum floors, carpets and furniture regularly, especially in the areas that the dog frequents, and wash the dog's bedding weekly.
- Follow up house-cleaning with carpet shampoos and sprays to rid the house of fleas at all stages of development. Insect growth regulators are the safest option.

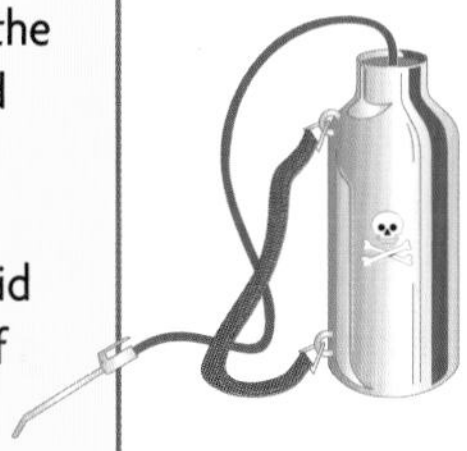

THE FLEA'S LIFE CYCLE

What came first, the flea or the egg? This age-old mystery is more difficult to comprehend than the actual cycle of the flea. Fleas usually live only about four months. A female can lay 2,000 eggs in her lifetime.

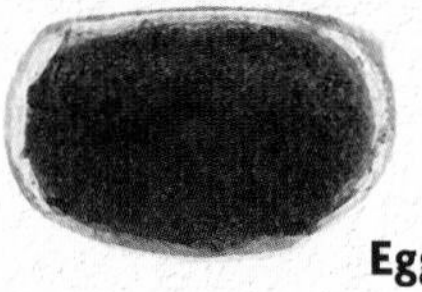

Egg

After ten days of rolling around your carpet or under your furniture, the eggs hatch into larvae, which feed on various and sundry debris. In days or months, depending on the climate, the larvae spin cocoons and develop into the pupal or nymph stage, which quickly develop into fleas.

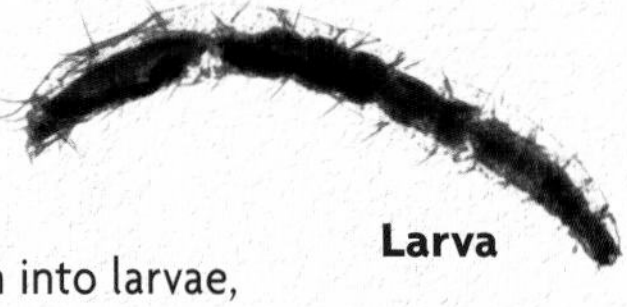

Larva

Pupa

These immature fleas must locate a host within 10 to 14 days or they will die. Only about 1% of the flea population exist as adult fleas, while the other 99% exist as eggs, larvae or pupae.

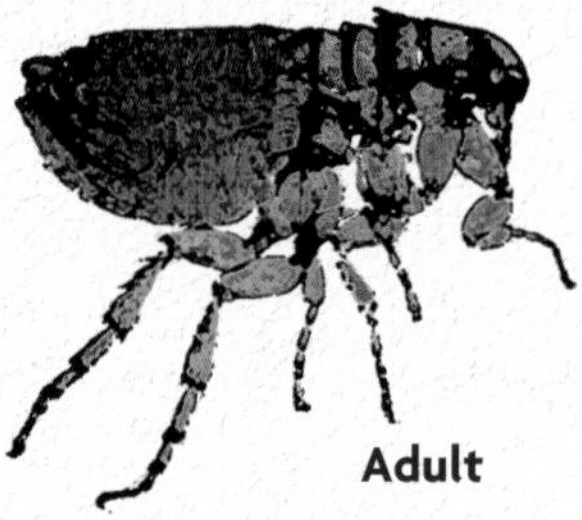

Adult

Photo by Carolina Biological Supply Co.

KILL FLEAS THE NATURAL WAY

If you choose not to go the route of conventional medication, there are some natural ways to ward off fleas:

- Dust your dog with a natural flea powder, composed of such herbal goodies as rosemary, wormwood, pennyroyal, citronella, rue, tobacco powder and eucalyptus.
- Apply diatomaceous earth, the fossilized remains of single-cell algae, to your carpets, furniture and pet's bedding. Even though it's not good for dogs, it's even worse for fleas, which will dry up swiftly and die.
- Brush your dog frequently, give him adequate exercise and let him fast occasionally. All of these activities strengthen the dog's system and make him more resistant to disease and parasites.
- Bathe your dog with a capful of pennyroyal or eucalyptus oil.
- Feed a natural diet, free of additives and preservatives. Add some fresh garlic and brewer's yeast to the dog's morning portion, as these items have flea-repelling properties.

the environment (e.g., pyriproxyfen, methoprene, fenoxycarb) as well as insect development inhibitors such as lufenuron that can be administered. These compounds have no effect on adult fleas, but they stop immature forms from developing into adults. In years gone by, we relied heavily on toxic insecticides (such as organophosphates, organochlorines and carbamates) to manage the flea problem, but today's options are not only much safer to use on our pets but also safer for the environment.

TICKS

Ticks are members of the spider class (arachnids) and are blood-sucking parasites capable of transmitting a variety of diseases, including Lyme disease, ehrlichiosis, babesiosis and Rocky Mountain spotted fever. It's easy to see ticks on your own skin, but it is more of a challenge when your furry companion is affected. Whenever you happen to be planning a stroll in a tick-infested area (especially forests, grassy or wooded areas or parks) be prepared to do a thorough inspection of your dog afterward to search for ticks. Ticks can be tricky, so make sure you spend time looking in the ears, between the toes and everywhere else where a tick might hide. Ticks need to be attached for 24–72 hours before they transmit most of the diseases that they carry, so you do have a window of opportunity for some preventive intervention.

A TICKING BOMB

There is nothing good about a tick's harpooning his nose into your dog's skin. Among the diseases caused by ticks are Rocky Mountain spotted fever, canine ehrlichiosis, canine babesiosis, canine hepatozoonosis and Lyme disease. If a dog is allergic to the saliva of a female wood tick, he can develop tick paralysis.

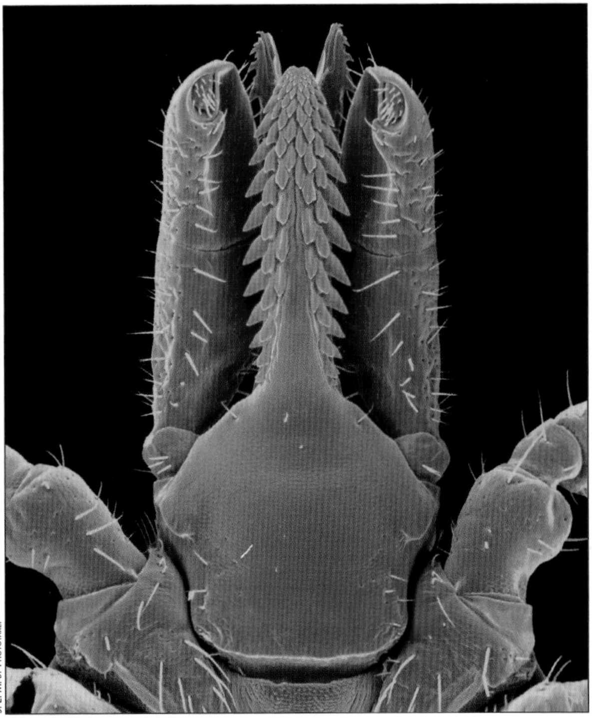

S. E. M. BY PHOTOTAKE.

A scanning electron micrograph of the head of a female deer tick, *Ixodes dammini*, a parasitic tick that carries Lyme disease.

Female ticks live to eat and breed. They can lay between 4,000 and 5,000 eggs and they die soon after. Males, on the other hand, live only to mate with the females and continue the process as long as they are able. Most ticks live on multiple hosts before parasitizing dogs. The immature forms typically reside on grass and shrubs, waiting for susceptible animals to walk by. The larvae and nymph stages typically feed on wildlife.

If only a few ticks are present on a dog, they can be plucked out, but it is important to remove the entire head and mouthparts,

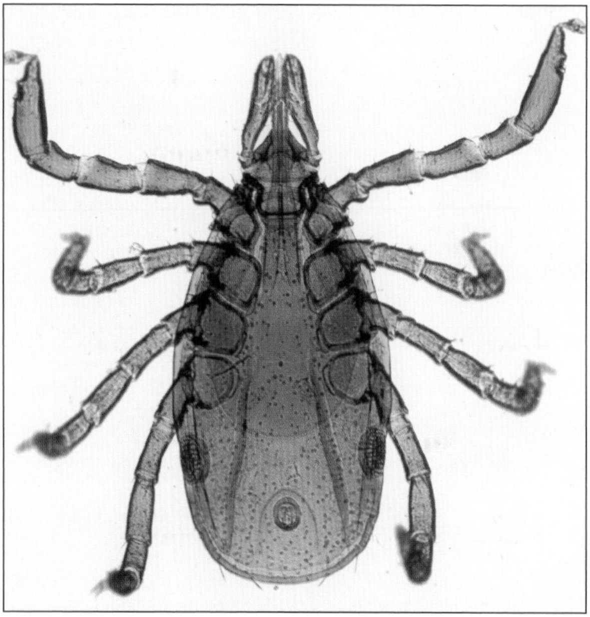

Deer tick, *Ixodes dammini.*

which may be deeply embedded in the skin. This is best accomplished with forceps designed especially for this purpose; fingers can be used but should be protected with rubber gloves, plastic wrap or at least a paper towel. The tick should be grasped as closely as possible to the animal's skin and should be pulled upward with steady, even pressure. Do not squeeze, crush or puncture the body of the tick or you risk exposure to any disease carried by that tick. Once the ticks have been removed, the sites of attachment should be disinfected. Your hands should then be washed with soap and water to further minimize risk of contagion. The tick should be disposed of in a container of alcohol or household bleach.

Some of the newer flea products, specifically those with fipronil, selamectin and permethrin, have effect against some, but not all, species of tick. Flea collars containing appropriate pesticides (e.g., propoxur, chlorfenvinphos) can aid in tick control. In most areas, such collars should be placed on animals in March, at the beginning of the tick season, and changed regularly. Leaving the collar on when the pesticide level is waning invites the development of resistance. Amitraz collars are also good for tick control, and the active ingredient does not interfere with other flea-control products. The ingredient helps prevent the attachment of ticks to the skin and will cause those ticks already on the skin to detach themselves.

TICK CONTROL

Removal of underbrush and leaf litter and the thinning of trees in areas where tick control is desired are recommended. These actions remove the cover and food sources for small animals that serve as hosts for ticks. With continued mowing of grasses in these areas, the probability of ticks' surviving is further reduced. A variety of insecticide ingredients (e.g., resmethrin, carbaryl, permethrin, chlorpyrifos, dioxathion and allethrin) are registered for tick control around the home.

Mites

Mites are tiny arachnid parasites that parasitize the skin of dogs. Skin diseases caused by mites are referred to as "mange," and there are many different forms seen in dogs. These forms are very different from one another, each one warranting an individual description.

Sarcoptic mange, or scabies, is one of the itchiest conditions that affects dogs. The microscopic *Sarcoptes* mites burrow into the superficial layers of the skin and can drive dogs crazy with itchiness. They are also communicable to people, although they can't complete their reproductive cycle on people. In addition to being tiny, the mites also are often difficult to find when trying to make a diagnosis. Skin scrapings from multiple areas are examined microscopically but, even then, sometimes the mites cannot be found.

Fortunately, scabies is relatively easy to treat, and there are a variety of products that will successfully kill the mites. Since the mites can't live in the environment for very long without feeding, a complete cure is usually possible within four to eight weeks.

Cheyletiellosis is caused by a relatively large mite, which sometimes can be seen even without a microscope. Often referred to as "walking dandruff," this also causes itching, but not usually as profound as with scabies. While *Cheyletiella* mites can survive somewhat longer in the environment than scabies mites, they too are relatively easy to treat, being responsive to not only the medications used to treat scabies but also often to flea-control products.

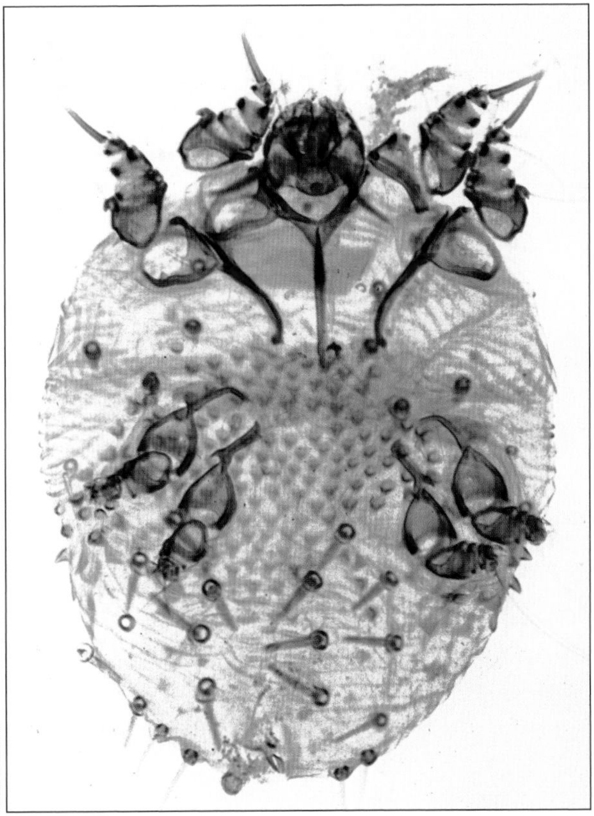

Photo by Phototake.

***Sarcoptes scabiei*, commonly known as the "itch mite."**

Otodectes cynotis is the canine ear mite and is one of the more common causes of mange, especially in young dogs in shelters or pet stores. That's because the mites are typically present in large numbers and are quickly spread to nearby animals. The mites rarely do much harm but

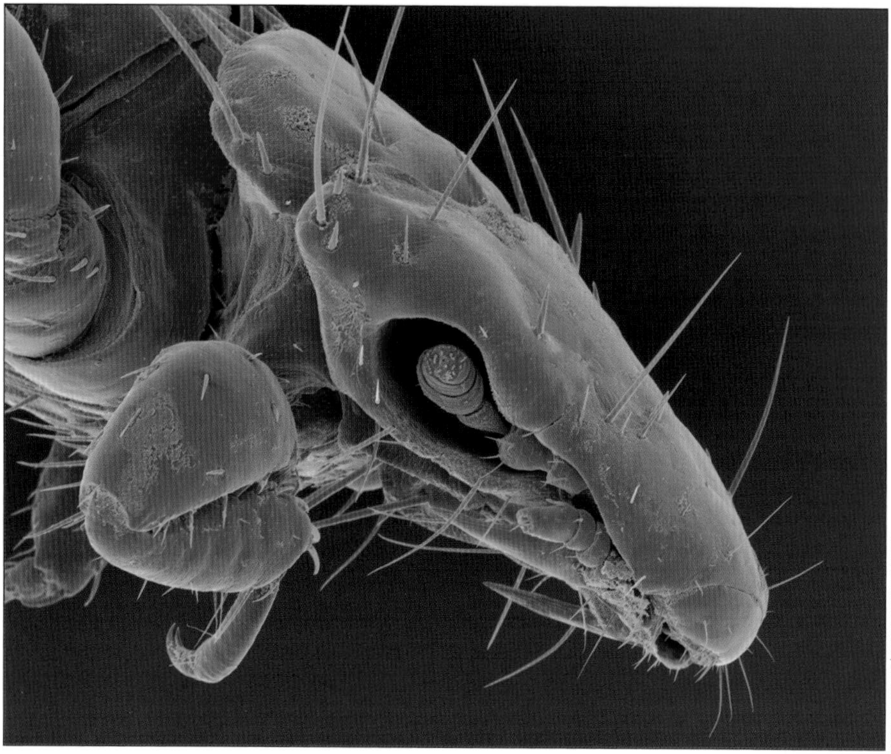

S. E. M. by Dr. Dennis Kunkel, University of Hawaii.

Micrograph of a dog louse, *Heterodoxus spiniger*. Female lice attach their eggs to the hairs of the dog. As the eggs hatch, the larval lice bite and feed on the blood. Lice can also feed on dead skin and hair. This feeding activity can cause hair loss and skin problems.

can be difficult to eradicate if the treatment regimen is not comprehensive. While many try to treat the condition with ear drops only, this is the most common cause of treatment failure. Ear drops cause the mites to simply move out of the ears and as far away as possible (usually to the base of the tail) until the insecticide levels in the ears drop to an acceptable level—then it's back to business as usual! The successful treatment of ear mites requires treating all animals in the household with a systemic insecticide, such as selamectin, or a combination of miticidal ear drops combined with whole-body flea-control preparations.

Demodicosis, sometimes referred to as red mange, can be one of the most difficult forms of mange to treat. Part of the problem has to do with the fact that the mites live in the hair follicles and they are relatively well shielded from topical and systemic products. The main issue, however, is that demodectic mange typically results only when there is some underlying process interfering with the dog's immune system.

Since *Demodex* mites are normal residents of the skin of

mammals, including humans, there is usually a mite population explosion only when the immune system fails to keep the number of mites in check. In young animals, the immune deficit may be transient or may reflect an actual inherited immune problem. In older animals, demodicosis is usually seen only when there is another disease hampering the immune system, such as diabetes, cancer, thyroid problems or the use of immune-suppressing drugs. Accordingly, treatment involves not only trying to kill the mange mites but also discerning what is interfering with immune function and correcting it if possible.

ILLUSTRATION BY PHOTOTAKE.

Illustration of *Demodex folliculoram.*

Chiggers represent several different species of mite that don't parasitize dogs specifically, but do latch on to passersby and can cause irritation. The problem is most prevalent in wooded areas in the late summer and fall. Treatment is not difficult, as the mites do not complete their life cycle on dogs and are susceptible to a variety of miticidal products.

MOSQUITOES

Mosquitoes have long been known to transmit a variety of diseases to people, as well as just being biting pests during warm weather. They also pose a real risk to pets. Not only do they carry deadly heartworms but recently there also has been much concern over their involvement with West Nile virus. While we can avoid heartworm with the use of preventive medications, there are no such preventives for West Nile virus. The only method of prevention in endemic areas is active mosquito control. Fortunately, most dogs that have been exposed to the virus only developed flu-like symptoms and, to date, there have not been the large number of reported deaths in canines as seen in some other species.

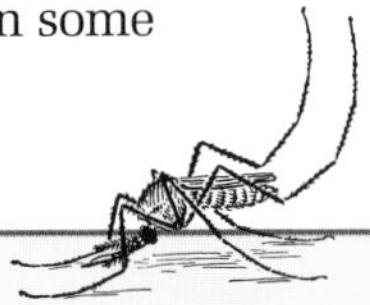

MOSQUITO REPELLENT

Low concentrations of DEET (less than 10%), found in many human mosquito repellents, have been safely used in dogs but, in these concentrations, probably give only about two hours of protection. DEET may be safe in these small concentrations, but since it is not licensed for use on dogs, there is no research proving its safety for dogs. Products containing permethrin give the longest-lasting protection, perhaps two to four weeks. As DEET is not licensed for use on dogs, and both DEET and permethrin can be quite toxic to cats, appropriate care should be exercised. Other products, such as those containing oil of citronella, also have some mosquito-repellent activity, but typically have a relatively short duration of action.

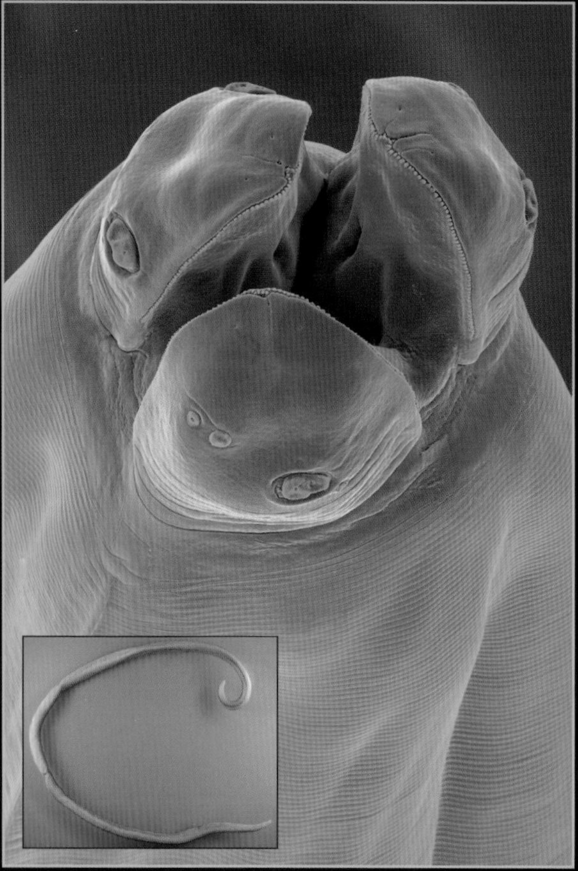

S. E. M. by Dr. Dennis Kunkel, University of Hawaii; Inset by Tam C. Nguyen.

The ascarid roundworm *Toxocara canis,* showing the mouth with three lips. INSET: Photomicrograph of the roundworm *Ascaris lumbricoides.*

ASCARID DANGERS

The most commonly encountered worms in dogs are roundworms known as ascarids. *Toxascaris leonine* and *Toxocara canis* are the two species that infect dogs. Subsisting in the dog's stomach and intestines, adult roundworms can grow to 7 inches in length and adult females can lay in excess of 200,000 eggs in a single day.

In humans, visceral larval migrans affects people who have ingested eggs of *Toxocara canis,* which frequently contaminates children's sandboxes, beaches and park grounds. The roundworms reside in the human's stomach and intestines, as they would in a dog's, but do not mature. Instead, they find their way to the liver, lungs and skin, or even to the heart or kidneys in severe cases. Deworming puppies is critical in preventing the infection in humans, and young children should never handle nursing pups who have not been dewormed.

INTERNAL PARASITES: WORMS

Ascarids

Ascarids are intestinal roundworms that rarely cause severe disease in dogs. Nonetheless, they are of major public health significance because they can be transferred to people. Sadly, it is children who are most commonly affected by the parasite, probably from inadvertently ingesting ascarid-contaminated soil. In fact, many yards and children's sandboxes contain appreciable numbers of ascarid eggs. So, while ascarids don't bite dogs or latch onto their intestines to suck blood, they do cause some nasty medical conditions in children and are best eradicated from our furry friends. Because pups can start passing ascarid eggs by three weeks of age, most parasite-control programs begin at two weeks of age and are repeated every two weeks until pups are eight weeks old. It is important to

HOOKED ON *ANCYLOSTOMA*

Adult dogs can become infected by the bloodsucking nematodes we commonly call hookworms via ingesting larvae from the ground or via the larvae penetrating the dog's skin. It is not uncommon for infected dogs to show no symptoms of hookworm infestation. Sometimes symptoms occur within ten days of exposure. These symptoms can include bloody diarrhea, anemia, loss of weight and general weakness. Dogs pass the hookworm eggs in their stools, which serves as the vet's method of identifying the infestation. The hookworm larvae can encyst themselves in the dog's tissues and be released when the dog is experiencing stress.

Caused by an *Ancylostoma* species whose common host is the dog, cutaneous larval migrans affects humans, causing itching and lumps and streaks beneath the surface of the skin.

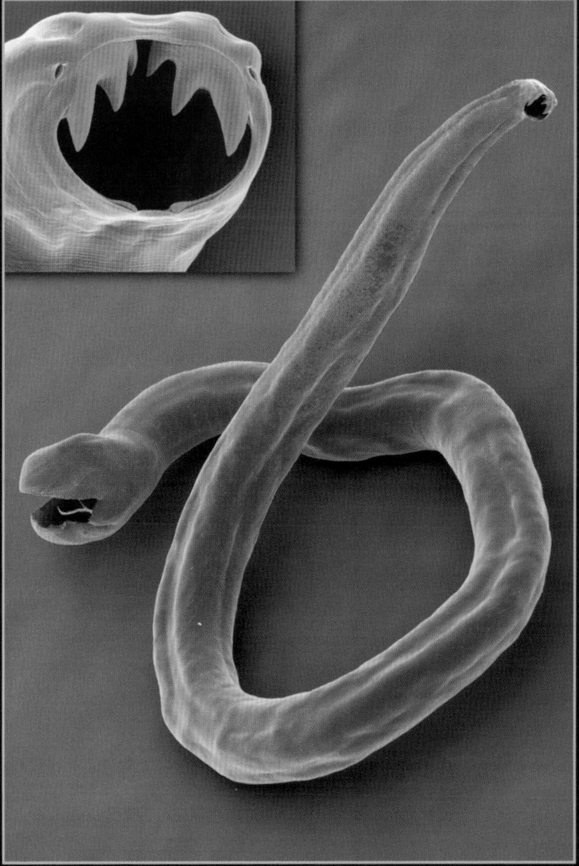

S. E. M. by Dr. Dennis Kunkel, University of Hawaii.

realize that bitches can pass ascarids to their pups even if they test negative prior to whelping. Accordingly, bitches are best treated at the same time as the pups.

HOOKWORMS

Unlike ascarids, hookworms do latch onto a dog's intestinal tract and can cause significant loss of blood and protein. Similar to ascarids, hookworms can be transmitted to humans, where they cause a condition known as cutaneous larval migrans. Dogs can become infected either by consuming the infective larvae or by the larvae's penetrating the skin directly. People most often get infected when they are lying on the ground (such as on a beach) and the larvae penetrate the skin. Yes, the larvae can penetrate through a beach blanket. Hookworms are typically susceptible to the same medications used to treat ascarids.

The hookworm *Ancylostoma caninum* infests the intestines of dogs. INSET: Note the row of hooks at the posterior end, used to anchor the worm to the intestinal wall.

Whipworms

Whipworms latch onto the lower aspects of the dog's colon and can cause cramping and diarrhea. Eggs do not start to appear in the dog's feces until about three months after the dog was infected. This worm has a peculiar life cycle, which makes it more difficult to control than ascarids or hookworms. The good thing is that whipworms rarely are transferred to people.

Some of the medications used to treat ascarids and hookworms are also effective against whipworms, but, in general, a separate treatment protocol is needed. Since most of the medications are effective against the adults but not the eggs or larvae, treatment is typically repeated in three weeks, and then often in three months as well. Unfortunately, since dogs don't develop resistance to whipworms, it is difficult to prevent them from getting reinfected if they visit soil contaminated with whipworm eggs.

Adult whipworm, *Trichuris* sp., an intestinal parasite.

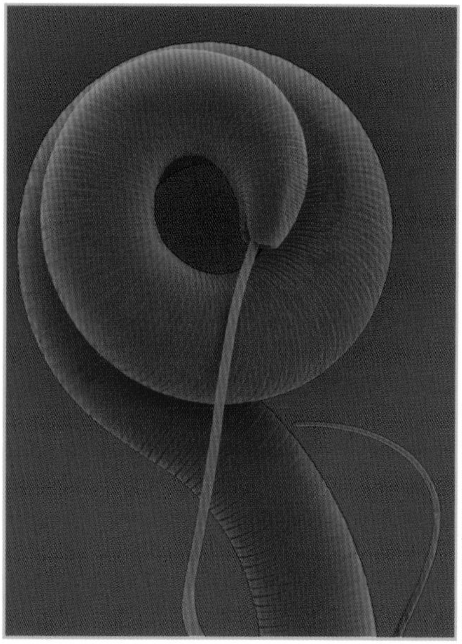

S. E. M. by Dr. Dennis Kunkel, University of Hawaii.

WORM-CONTROL GUIDELINES

- Practice sanitary habits with your dog and home.
- Clean up after your dog and don't let him sniff or eat other dogs' droppings.
- Control insects and fleas in the dog's environment. Fleas, lice, cockroaches, beetles, mice and rats can act as hosts for various worms.
- Prevent dogs from eating uncooked meat, raw poultry and dead animals.
- Keep dogs and children from playing in sand and soil.
- Kennel dogs on cement or gravel; avoid dirt runs.
- Administer heartworm preventives regularly.
- Have your vet examine your dog's stools at your annual visits.
- Select a boarding kennel carefully so as to avoid contamination from other dogs or an unsanitary environment.
- Prevent dogs from roaming. Obey local leash laws.

Tapeworms

There are many different species of tapeworm that affect dogs, but *Dipylidium caninum* is probably the most common and is spread by fleas. Flea larvae feed on organic debris and tapeworm eggs in the environment and, when a dog chews at himself and manages to ingest fleas, he might get a dose of tapeworm at the same time. The tapeworm then develops further in the intestine of the dog.

The tapeworm itself, which latches onto the intestinal wall, is composed of numerous segments. When the segments break off into the intestine (as proglottids), they may accumulate around the rectum, like grains of rice. While this tapeworm is disgusting in its behavior, it is not directly communicable to humans (although humans can also get infected by swallowing fleas).

S. E. M. by Dr. Dennis Kunkel, University of Hawaii.

A dog tapeworm proglottid (body segment).

A much more dangerous flatworm is *Echinococcus multilocularis*, which is typically found in foxes, coyotes and wolves. The eggs are passed in the feces and infect rodents, and, when dogs eat the rodents, the dogs can be infected by thousands of adult tapeworms. While the parasites don't cause many problems in dogs, this is considered the most lethal worm infection that people can get. Take appropriate precautions if you live in an area in which these tapeworms are found. Do not use mulch that may contain feces of dogs, cats or wildlife, and discourage your pets from hunting wildlife. Treat these tapeworm infections aggressively in pets, because if humans get infected, approximately half die.

Heartworms

Heartworm disease is caused by the parasite *Dirofilaria immitis* and is seen in dogs around the world. A member of the roundworm group, it is spread between dogs by the bite of an infected mosquito. The mosquito injects infective larvae into the dog's skin with its bite, and these larvae develop under the skin for a period of time before making their way to the heart. There they develop into adults, which grow and create blockages of the heart, lungs and major blood vessels there. They also start producing offspring (microfilariae)

S. E. M. by Dr. Dennis Kunkel, University of Hawaii.

The dog tapeworm *Taenia pisiformis*.

A Look at Internal Parasites

Photo by Carolina Biological Supply Co.

Ascarid *Rhabditis*

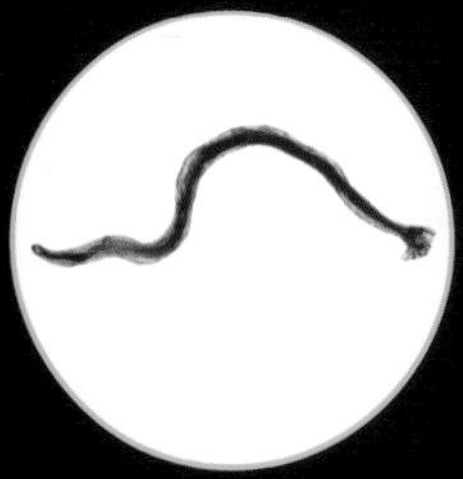

Photo by Carolina Biological Supply Co.

Hookworm *Ancylostoma caninum*

Photo by Tam C. Nguyen.

Tapeworm *Dipylidium caninum*

Photo by Tam C. Nguyen.

Heartworm *Dirofilaria immitis*

and these microfilariae circulate in the bloodstream, waiting to hitch a ride when the next mosquito bites. Once in the mosquito, the microfilariae develop into infective larvae and the entire process is repeated.

When dogs get infected with heartworm, over time they tend to develop symptoms associated with heart disease, such as coughing, exercise intolerance and potentially many other manifestations. Diagnosis is confirmed by either seeing the microfilariae themselves in blood samples or using immunologic tests (antigen testing) to identify the presence of adult heartworms. Since antigen tests measure the presence of adult heartworms and microfilarial tests measure offspring produced by adults, neither are positive until six to seven months after the initial infection. However, the beginning of damage can occur by fifth-stage larvae as early as three months after infection. Thus it is possible for dogs to be harboring problem-causing larvae for up to three months before either type of test would identify an infection.

The good news is that there are great protocols available for preventing heartworm in dogs. Testing is critical in the process, and it is important to understand the benefits as well as the limitations of such testing. All dogs six months of age or older that have not been on continuous heartworm-preventive medication

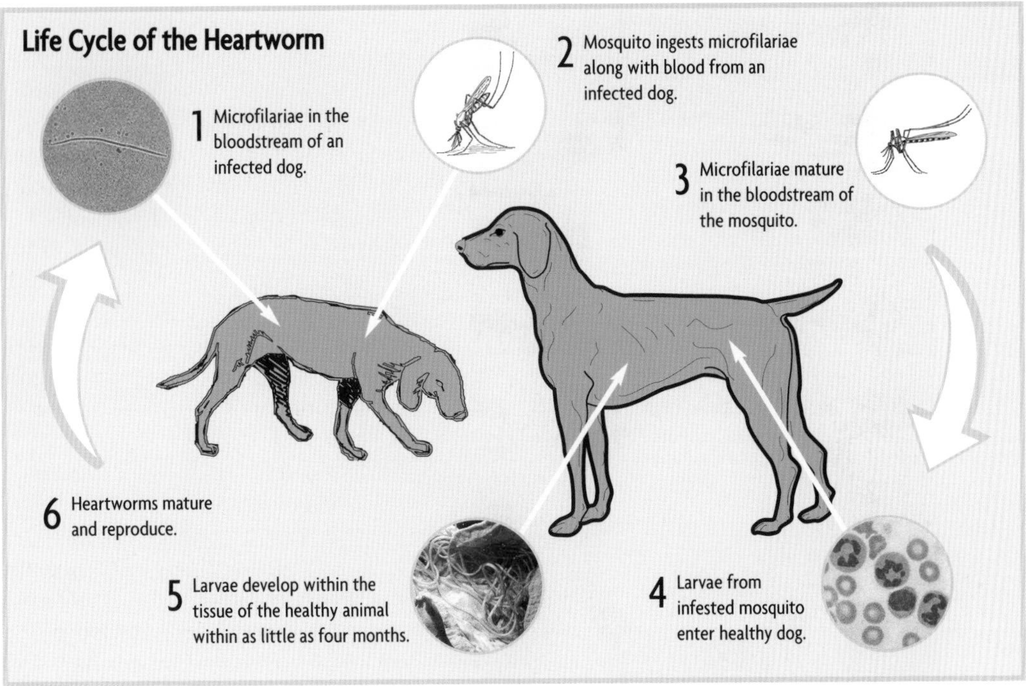

should be screened with microfilarial or antigen tests. For dogs receiving preventive medication, periodic antigen testing helps assess the effectiveness of the preventives. The American Heartworm Society guidelines suggest that annual retesting may not be necessary when owners have absolutely provided continuous heartworm prevention. Retesting on a two- to three-year interval may be sufficient in these cases. However, your veterinarian will likely have specific guidelines under which heartworm preventives will be prescribed, and many prefer to err on the side of safety and retest annually.

It is indeed fortunate that heartworm is relatively easy to prevent, because treatments can be as life-threatening as the disease itself. Treatment requires a two-step process that kills the adult heartworms first and then the microfilariae. Prevention is obviously preferable; this involves a once-monthly oral or topical treatment. The most common oral preventives include ivermectin (not suitable for some breeds), moxidectin and milbemycin oxime; the once-a-month topical drug selamectin provides heartworm protection in addition to flea, tick and other parasite controls.

CDS: Cognitive Dysfunction Syndrome

"Old-Dog Syndrome"

There are many ways for you to evaluate old-dog syndrome. Veterinarians have defined CDS (cognitive dysfunction syndrome) as the gradual deterioration of cognitive abilities, indicated by changes in the dog's behavior. When a dog changes his routine response, and maladies have been eliminated as the cause of these behavioral changes, then CDS is the usual diagnosis.

More than half the dogs over eight years old suffer from some form of CDS. The older the dog, the more chance he has of suffering from CDS. In humans, doctors often dismiss the CDS behavioral changes as part of "winding down."

There are four major signs of CDS: frequent potty accidents inside the home, sleeping much more or much less than normal, acting confused and failing to respond to social stimuli.

Symptoms of CDS

FREQUENT POTTY ACCIDENTS

- Urinates in the house.
- Defecates in the house.
- Doesn't signal that he wants to go out.

FAILURE TO RESPOND TO SOCIAL STIMULI

- Comes to people less frequently, whether called or not.
- Doesn't tolerate petting for more than a short time.
- Doesn't come to the door when you return home.

CONFUSION

- Goes outside and just stands there.
- Appears confused with a faraway look in his eyes.
- Hides more often.
- Doesn't recognize friends.
- Doesn't come when called.
- Walks around listlessly and without a destination.

SLEEP PATTERNS

- Awakens more slowly.
- Sleeps more than normal during the day.
- Sleeps less during the night.

YOUR SENIOR AUSTRALIAN TERRIER

When we bring home a puppy, full of the energy and exuberance that accompanies youth, we hope for a long, happy and fulfilling relationship with the new family member. Even when we adopt an older dog, we look forward to the years of companionship ahead with a new canine friend. However, aging is inevitable for all creatures, and there will come a time when your Australian Terrier reaches his senior years and will need special considerations and attention to his care.

WHEN IS MY DOG A "SENIOR"?

In general, pure-bred dogs are considered to have achieved senior status when they reach 75% of their breed's average lifespan, with lifespan being based on breed size. Your hardy Australian Terrier has an average lifespan of 12 or more years, so can be considered a senior citizen at around age nine.

Obviously, the old "seven dog years to one human year" theory is not exact. In puppyhood, a dog's year is actually comparable to more than seven human years, considering the puppy's rapid growth during his first year. Then, in adulthood, the ratio decreases. Regardless, the more viable rule of thumb is that the larger the dog, the shorter his expected lifespan. Of course, this can vary among individual dogs, with many living longer than expected, which we hope is the case!

WHAT ARE THE SIGNS OF AGING?

By the time your dog has reached his senior years, you will know him very well, so the physical and behavioral changes that accompany aging should be noticeable to you. Humans and dogs share the most obvious physical sign of aging: gray hair! Graying often occurs first on the muzzle and face, around the eyes. Other telltale signs are the dog's overall decrease in activity. Your older dog might be more content to nap and rest, and he may not show the same old enthusiasm when it's time to play in the yard or go for a walk.

Other physical signs include significant weight loss or gain; more labored movement; skin and coat problems, possibly hair loss; sight and/or hearing problems; changes in toileting habits, perhaps seeming "unhousebroken" at times; and tooth decay, bad breath or other mouth problems.

There are behavioral changes that go along with aging, too. There are numerous causes for behavioral changes. Sometimes a dog's apparent confusion results from a physical change like diminished sight or hearing. If his confusion causes him to be afraid, he may act aggressively or defensively. He may sleep more frequently because his daily walks, though shorter now, tire him out. He may begin to experience separation anxiety or, conversely, become less interested in petting and attention.

There also are clinical conditions that cause behavioral changes in older dogs. One such condition is known as cognitive dysfunction (familiarly known as "old-dog" syndrome). It can be frustrating for an owner whose dog is affected with cognitive dysfunction, as it can result in behavioral changes of all types, most seemingly unexplainable. Common changes include the dog's forgetting aspects of the daily routine, such as times to eat, go out for walks, relieve himself and the like. Along the same lines, you may take your dog out at the regular time for a potty trip and he may have no idea why he is there. Sometimes a placid dog will begin to show aggressive or possessive tendencies or, conversely, a hyperactive dog will start to "mellow out."

Disease also can be the cause of behavioral changes in senior dogs. Hormonal problems (Cushing's disease is common in older dogs), diabetes and thyroid disease can cause increased appetite, which can lead to aggression related to food guarding. It's better to be proactive with your senior dog, making more frequent trips to the vet if necessary and having bloodwork done to test for the diseases that can commonly befall older dogs.

This is not to say that, as dogs age, they all fall apart physically and become nasty in personality. The aforementioned changes are discussed to alert owners to the things that may happen as their dogs get older. Many hardy dogs remain active and alert well into old age. However, it can be frustrating and heartbreaking for owners to see their beloved dogs change physically and temperamentally. Just know that it's the same Australian Terrier under there, and that he still loves you and appreciates your care, which he needs now more than ever.

HOW DO I CARE FOR MY AGING DOG?

Even if your dog shows no outward signs of aging, he should begin a senior-care program once he reaches the determined age. By providing him with extra attention to his veterinary care at this age, you will be practicing good preventive medicine, ensuring that the rest of your dog's life will be as long, active, happy and healthy as possible. If you do notice indications of aging, such as graying and/or changes in sleeping, eating or toileting habits, this is a sign to set up a senior-care visit with your vet right away to make sure that these changes are not related to any health problems.

To start, senior dogs should visit the vet twice yearly for exams, routine tests and overall evaluations. Many veterinarians have special screening programs especially for senior dogs that can include a thorough physical exam; blood test to determine complete blood count; serum biochemistry test, which screens for liver, kidney and blood problems as well as cancer; urinalysis; and dental exams. With these tests, it can be determined whether your dog has any health problems; the results also establish a baseline for your pet against which future test results can be compared.

In addition to these tests, your vet may suggest additional testing, including an EKG, tests for glaucoma and other problems of the eye, chest X-rays, screening for tumors, blood pressure test, test for thyroid function and screening for parasites and reassessment of his preventive program. Your vet also will ask you questions about your dog's diet and activity level, what you feed and the amounts that you feed. This information, along with his evaluation of the dog's overall condition, will enable him to suggest proper dietary changes, if needed.

ADAPTING TO AGE

As dogs age and their once-keen senses begin to deteriorate, they can experience stress and confusion. However, dogs are very adaptable, and most can adjust to deficiencies in their sight and hearing. As these processes often deteriorate gradually, the dog makes adjustments gradually, too. Because dogs become so familiar with the layout of their homes and yards, and with their daily routines, they are able to get around even if they cannot see or hear as well. Help your senior dog by keeping things consistent around the house. Keep up with your regular times for walking and potty trips, and do not relocate his crate or rearrange the furniture. Your dog is a very adaptable creature and can make compensation for his diminished ability, but you want to help him along the way and not make changes that will cause him confusion.

This may seem like quite a work-up for your pet, but veterinarians advise that older dogs need more frequent attention so that any health problems can be detected as early as possible. Serious conditions like kidney disease, heart disease and cancer may not present outward symptoms, or the problem may go undetected if the symptoms are mistaken by owners as just part of the aging process.

There are some conditions more common in elderly dogs that are difficult to ignore. Cognitive dysfunction shares much in common with senility and Alzheimer's disease, and dogs are not immune. Dogs can become confused and/or disoriented, lose their house-training, have abnormal sleep-wake cycles and interact differently with their owners. Be heartened by the fact that, in some ways, there are more treatment options for dogs with cognitive dysfunction than for people with similar conditions. There is good evidence that continued stimulation in the form of games, play, training and exercise can help to maintain cognitive function. There are also medications (such as seligiline) and antioxidant-fortified senior diets that have been shown to be beneficial.

Cancer is also a condition more common in the elderly. Almost all of the cancers seen in people are also seen in pets. If pets are getting regular physical examinations, cancers are often detected early. There are a variety of cancer therapies available today, and many pets continue to live happy lives with appropriate treatment.

Arthritis is another malady common to both elderly dogs and humans. A lifetime of wear and tear on joints and running around at play eventually takes its toll and results in stiffness and difficulty in getting around. As dogs live longer and healthier lives, it is natural that they should eventually feel some of the effects of aging. Once again, if regular veterinary care has been given, your pet should not have been carrying extra pounds all those years and wearing those joints out before their time. If your pet was unfortunate enough to inherit hip dysplasia, osteochondrosis dissecans or any of the other developmental orthopedic diseases, battling the onset of degenerative joint disease was probably a longstanding goal. In any case, there are now many effective remedies for managing degenerative joint disease and a number of remarkable surgeries as well.

Aside from the extra veterinary care, there is much you can do at home to keep your older dog in good condition. The dog's diet is an important factor. If your dog's appetite decreases, he will not be getting the nutrients he needs. He also will lose weight, which is unhealthy for a dog at a proper weight. Conversely, an older dog's metabolism is slower and he usually exercises less, but he should not be allowed to become obese. Obesity in an older dog is especially risky, because extra pounds mean extra stress on the body, increasing his vulnerability to heart disease. Additionally, the extra pounds make it harder for the dog to move about.

You should discuss age-related feeding changes with your vet. For a dog who has lost interest in food, it may be suggested to try some different types of food until you find something new that the dog likes. For an obese dog, a "light" formula dog food or reducing food portions may be advised, along with exercise appropriate to his physical condition and energy level.

The senior dog should not be allowed to become a "couch potato" despite his old age. He may not be able to handle the morning run, long walks and vigorous games of fetch, but he still needs to get up and get moving. Keep up with your daily walks, but keep the distances shorter and let your dog set the pace. If he gets to the point where he's not up for walks, let him stroll around the yard. On the other hand, many dogs remain very active in their senior years, so base changes to the exercise program on your own individual dog and what he's capable of. Don't worry, your Australian Terrier will let you know when it's time to rest.

Keep up with your grooming and be extra-diligent about checking the skin and coat for problems. Older dogs can experience thinning coats as a normal process, but they can also lose hair as a result of medical problems. Some thinning is normal, but patches of baldness or significant hair loss is not.

Hopefully, you've been regular with brushing your dog's teeth throughout his life. Healthy teeth directly affect overall good health. We already know that bacteria from gum infections can enter the dog's body through the damaged gums and travel to the organs. At a stage in life when his organs don't function as well as they used to, you don't want anything to put additional strain on them. Clean teeth also contribute to a healthy immune system. Offering the dental-type chews in addition to toothbrushing can help, as they remove plaque and tartar as the dog chews.

Along with the same good care you've given him all of his life, pay a little extra attention to your dog in his senior years and keep up with twice-yearly trips to the vet. The sooner a problem is uncovered, the greater the chances of a full recovery.

SHOWING YOUR
AUSTRALIAN TERRIER

Is dog showing in your blood? Are you excited by the idea of gaiting your handsome Australian Terrier around the ring to the thunderous applause of an enthusiastic audience? Are you certain that your beloved Australian Terrier is flawless? You are not alone! Every loving owner thinks that his dog has no faults, or too few to mention. No matter how many times an owner reads the breed standard, he cannot find any faults in his aristocratic companion dog. If this sounds like you, and if you are considering entering your Australian Terrier in a dog show, here are some basic questions to ask yourself:

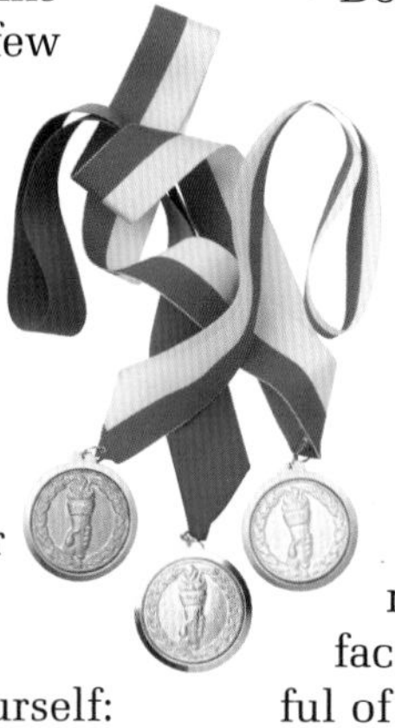

- Did you purchase a "show-quality" puppy from the breeder?
- Is your puppy at least six months of age?
- Does the puppy exhibit correct show type for his breed?
- Does your puppy have any disqualifying faults?
- Is your Aussie registered with the American Kennel Club?
- How much time do you have to devote to training, grooming, conditioning and exhibiting your dog?
- Do you understand the rules and regulations of a dog show?
- Do you have time to learn how to show your dog properly?
- Do you have the financial resources to invest in showing your dog?
- Will you show the dog yourself or hire a professional handler?
- Do you have a vehicle that can accommodate your weekend trips to the dog shows?

Success in the show ring requires more than a pretty face, a waggy tail and a pocketful of liver. Even though dog shows can be exciting and enjoyable, the sport of conformation makes great demands on the exhibitors and the dogs. Winning exhibitors live for their dogs, devoting time and money to their dogs' presentation, conditioning and training. Very few novices, even those with good dogs, will find themselves in the winners' circle, though it does happen. Don't be disheartened, though. Every exhibitor began as a novice and worked his way up to the Group ring. It's the "working your way up" part that you must keep in mind.

Assuming that you have purchased a puppy of the correct type and quality for showing, let's begin to examine the world of showing and what's required to get started. Although the entry fee into a dog show is nominal, there are lots of other hidden costs involved with "finishing" your Australian Terrier, that is, making him a champion. Things like equipment, travel, training and conditioning all cost money. A more serious campaign will include fees for a professional handler, boarding, cross-country travel and advertising. Top-winning show dogs can represent a very considerable investment—over $100,000 has been spent in campaigning some dogs. (The investment can be less, of course, for owners who don't use professional handlers.)

Many owners, on the other hand, enter their "average" Australian Terriers in dog shows for the fun and enjoyment of it. Dog showing makes an absorbing hobby, with many rewards for dogs and owners alike. If you're having fun, meeting other people who share your interests and enjoying the overall experience, you likely will catch the "bug." Once the dog-

SEAL OF EXCELLENCE

The show ring is the testing ground for a breeder's program. A championship on a dog signifies that three qualified judges have placed their seal of approval on a dog. Only dogs that have earned their championships should be considered for breeding purposes. Striving to improve the breed and reproduce sound, typical examples of the breed, breeders must breed only the best. No breeder breeds only for pet homes; they strive for the top. The goal of every program must be to better the breed, and every responsible breeder wants the prestige of producing Best in Show winners.

show bug bites, its effects can last a lifetime; it's certainly much better than a deer tick! Soon you will be envisioning yourself in the center ring at the Westminster Kennel Club Dog Show in New York City, competing for the prestigious Best in Show cup. This magical dog show is televised annually from Madison Square Garden, and the victorious dog becomes a celebrity overnight.

AKC CONFORMATION SHOWING

Getting Started

Visiting a dog show as a spectator is a great place to start. Pick up the show catalog to find out what time your breed is being shown, who is judging the breed and in which ring the classes will be held. To start, Australian Terriers compete against other Australian Terriers, and the winner is selected as Best of Breed by the judge. This is the procedure for each breed. At a group show, all of the Best of Breed winners go on to compete for Group One in their respective groups. For example, all Best of Breed winners in a given group compete against each other; this is done for all seven groups. Finally, all seven group winners go head to head in the ring for the Best in Show award.

What most spectators don't understand is the basic idea of conformation. A dog show is often referred as a "conformation" show. This means that the judge should decide how each dog stacks up (conforms) to the breed standard for his given breed: how well does this Australian Terrier conform to the ideal representative detailed in the standard? Ideally, this is what happens. In reality, however, this ideal often gets slighted as the judge compares Australian Terrier #1 to Australian Terrier #2. Again, the ideal is that each dog is judged based on his merits in comparison to his breed standard, not in comparison to the other dogs in the ring. It is easier for judges to compare dogs of the same breed to decide which they think is the better specimen; in the Group and Best in Show ring, however, it is very difficult to compare one breed to another, like apples to oranges. Thus the dog's conformation to the breed standard—not to mention advertising dollars and good handling—is essential to success in conformation shows. The dog described in the standard (the standard for each AKC breed is written and approved by the breed's national parent club and then submitted to the AKC for approval) is the perfect dog of that breed, and breeders keep their eye on the standard when they choose which dogs to breed, hoping to get closer and closer to the ideal with each litter.

Another good first step for the novice is to join a dog club. You

NATIONAL CLUBS

For reliable, up-to-date information about registration, dog shows and other canine competitions, contact one of the national registries by mail or via the Internet.

American Kennel Club
5580 Centerview Dr., Raleigh, NC 27606-3390
www.akc.org

United Kennel Club
100 E. Kilgore Road, Kalamazoo, MI 49002
www.ukcdogs.com

Canadian Kennel Club
89 Skyway Ave., Suite 100, Etobicoke, Ontario
M9W 6R4 Canada
www.ckc.ca

The Kennel Club
1-5 Clarges St., Piccadilly, London W1Y 8AB, UK
www.the-kennel-club.org.uk

will be astonished by the many and different kinds of dog clubs in the country, with about 5,000 clubs holding events every year. Most clubs require that prospective new members present two letters of recommendation from existing members. Perhaps you've made some friends visiting a show held by a particular club and you would like to join that club. Dog clubs may specialize in a single breed, like a local or regional Australian Terrier club, or in a specific pursuit, such as obedience, tracking or hunting tests. There are all-breed clubs for all dog enthusiasts; they sponsor special training days, seminars on topics like grooming or handling or lectures on breeding or canine genetics. There are also clubs that specialize in certain types of dogs, like herding dogs, hunting dogs, companion dogs, etc.

A parent club is the national organization, sanctioned by the AKC, which promotes and safeguards its breed in the country. The Australian Terrier Club of America was formed in 1957 and can be contacted on the Internet at www.australianterrier.org. The parent club holds an annual national specialty show, usually in a different city each year, in which many of the country's top dogs, handlers and breeders gather to compete. At a specialty

AKC GROUPS

For showing purposes, the American Kennel Club divides its recognized breeds into seven groups: Terriers, Sporting Dogs, Hounds, Working Dogs, Toys, Non-Sporting Dogs and Herding Dogs.

show, only members of a single breed are invited to participate. There are also group specialties, in which all members of a group are invited. For more information about dog clubs in your area, contact the AKC at www.akc.org on the Internet or write them at their Raleigh, NC address.

How Shows Are Organized

Three kinds of conformation shows are offered by the AKC. There is the all-breed show, in which all AKC-recognized breeds can compete; the specialty show, which is for one breed only and usually sponsored by the breed's parent club, and the Group show, for all breeds in one of the seven AKC groups. The Australian Terrier competes in the Terrier Group.

For a dog to become an AKC champion of record, the dog must earn 15 points at shows. The points must be awarded by at least three different judges and must include two "majors" under different judges. A "major" is a three-, four- or five-point win, and the number of points per win is determined by the number of dogs competing in the show on that day. (Dogs that are absent or are excused are not counted.) The number of points that are awarded varies from breed to breed. More dogs are needed to attain a major in more popular breeds, and fewer dogs are needed in less popular breeds. Yearly, the AKC evaluates the number of dogs in competition in each division (there are 14 divisions in all, based on geography) and may or may not change the numbers of dogs required for each number of points. For example, a major in Division 2 (Delaware, New Jersey and Pennsylvania) recently required 17 dogs or 16 bitches for a three-point major, 29 dogs or 27 bitches for a four-point major and 51 dogs or 46 bitches for a five-point major. The Australian Terrier attracts numerically proportionate representation at all-breed shows.

Only one dog and one bitch of each breed can win points at a given show. There are no "co-ed" classes except for champions of record. Dogs and bitches do not compete against each other until they are champions. Dogs that are not champions (referred to as "class dogs") compete in one of five classes. The class in which a dog is entered depends on age and previous show wins. First there is the Puppy Class (sometimes divided further into classes for 6- to 9-month-olds and 9- to 12-

month-olds); next is the Novice Class (for dogs that have no points toward their championships and whose only first-place wins have come in the Puppy Class or the Novice Class, the latter class limited to three first places); then there is the American-bred Class (for dogs bred in the US); the Bred-by-Exhibitor Class (for dogs handled by their breeders or by immediate family members of their breeders) and the Open Class (for any non-champions). Any dog may enter the Open class, regardless of age or win history, but to be competitive the dog should be older and have ring experience.

The judge at the show begins judging the male dogs in the Puppy Class(es) and proceeds through the other classes. The judge awards first through fourth place in each class. The first-place winners of each class then compete with one another in the Winners Class to determine Winners Dog. The judge then starts over with the bitches, beginning with the Puppy Class(es) and proceeding up to the Winners Class to award Winners Bitch, just as he did with the dogs. A Reserve Winners Dog and Reserve Winners Bitch are also selected; they could be awarded the points in the case of a disqualification.

The Winners Dog and Winners Bitch are the two that are awarded the points for their breed. They then go on to compete with any

ON THE MOVE

The truest test of a dog's proper structure is his gait, the way the dog moves. The American Kennel Club defines gait as "the pattern of footsteps at various rates of speed, each pattern distinguished by a particular rhythm and footfall." That the dog moves smoothly and effortlessly indicates to the judge that the dog's structure is well made. From the four-beat gallop, the fastest of canine gaits, to the high-lifting hackney gait, each breed varies in its correct gait; not every breed is expected to move in the same way. Each breed standard defines the correct gait for its breed and often identifies movement faults, such as toeing in, side-winding, over-reaching or crossing over.

champions of record (often called "specials") of their breed that are entered in the show. The champions may be dogs or bitches; in this class, all are shown together. The judge reviews the Winners Dog and Winners Bitch along with all of the champions to select the Best of Breed winner. The Best of Winners is selected between the Winners Dog and Winners Bitch; if one of these two is selected Best of Breed as well, he or she is automatically determined Best of Winners. Lastly, the judge selects Best of Opposite Sex to the Best of Breed winner. The Best of Breed winner then goes on to the group competition.

At a group or all-breed show, the Best of Breed winners from each breed are divided into their respective groups to compete against one another for Group One through Group Four. Group One (first place) is awarded to the dog that best lives up to the ideal for his breed as described in the standard. A group judge, therefore, must have a thorough working knowledge of many breed standards. After placements have been made in each group, the seven Group One winners (from the Sporting Group, Toy Group, Hound Group, etc.) compete against each other for the top honor, Best in Show.

There are different ways to find out about dog shows in your area. The American Kennel Club's monthly magazine, the *American Kennel Gazette* is accompanied by the *Events Calendar*; this magazine is available through subscription. You can also look on the AKC's and your parent club's websites for information and check the event listings in your local newspaper.

Your Australian Terrier must be six months of age or older and registered with the AKC in order to be entered in AKC-sanctioned shows in which there are classes for the Australian Terrier. Your Australian Terrier also must not possess any disqualifying faults and must be sexually intact. The reason for the latter is simple: dog shows are the proving grounds to determine which dogs and bitches are worthy of being bred. If they cannot be bred, that defeats the purpose! On that note, only dogs that have achieved championships, thus proving their excellent quality, should be bred. If you have spayed or neutered your dog, however, there are many AKC events other than conformation, such as obedience trials, agility trials and the Canine Good Citizen® program, in which you and your Australian Terrier can participate.

OTHER TYPES OF COMPETITION

In addition to conformation shows, the AKC holds a variety of other competitive events. Obedience trials, agility trials and tracking trials are open to all breeds, while hunting tests, field trials, lure coursing, herding tests and trials, earthdog tests and coonhound events are limited to specific breeds or groups of breeds. The Junior Showmanship program is offered to aspiring young handlers and their dogs, and the Canine Good Citizen® program is an all-around good-behavior test open to all dogs, pure-bred and mixed.

Obedience Trials

Mrs. Helen Whitehouse Walker, a Standard Poodle fancier, can be credited with introducing obedience trials to the United States. In the 1930s, she designed a series of exercises based on those of the Associated Sheep, Police, Army Dog Society of Great Britain. These exercises were intended to evaluate the working relationship between dog and owner. Since those early days of the sport in the US, obedience trials have grown more and more popular, and now more than 2,000 trials each year attract over 100,000 dogs and their owners. Any dog registered with the AKC, regardless of neutering or other disqualifications that would preclude entry in conformation competition, can participate in obedience trials.

There are three levels of difficulty in obedience competition. The first (and easiest) level is the Novice, in which dogs can earn the Companion Dog (CD) title. The intermediate level is the Open level, in which the Companion Dog Excellent (CDX) title is awarded. The advanced level is the Utility level, in which dogs compete for the Utility Dog (UD) title.

A dog must complete different exercises at each level of obedience. The Novice exercises are the easiest, with the Open and finally the Utility levels progressing in difficulty. Once he's earned the UD title, a dog can go on to win the prestigious title of Utility Dog Excellent (UDX) by winning "legs"

Because of their small size and go-to-ground mentality, the Australian Terrier does well in the tunnel at agility trials.

in ten shows. Additionally, Utility Dogs who win "legs" in Open B and Utility B earn points toward the lofty title of Obedience Trial Champion (OTCh.). The "brass ring" of obedience competition is the AKC's National Obedience Invitational. In order to qualify for the invitational, a dog must be ranked in either the top 25 all-breeds in obedience or in the top three for his breed in obedience. The title at stake here is that of National Obedience Champion (NOC).

Agility Trials

Agility trials became sanctioned by the AKC in August 1994, when the first licensed agility trials were held. Since that time, agility certainly has grown in popularity by leaps and bounds, literally! The AKC allows all registered breeds (including Miscellaneous Class breeds) to participate, providing the dog is 12 months of age or older. Agility is designed so that the handler demonstrates how well the dog can work at his side. The handler directs his dog through, over, under and around an obstacle course that includes jumps, tires, the dog walk, weave poles, pipe tunnels, collapsed tunnels and more. While working his way through the course, the dog must keep one eye and ear on the handler and the rest of his body on the course. The handler runs along with the dog, giving verbal and hand signals to guide the dog through the course.

The first organization to promote agility trials in the US was the United States Dog Agility Association, Inc. (USDAA). Established in 1986, the USDAA sparked the formation of many member clubs around the country. To participate in USDAA trials, dogs must be at least 18 months of age. The USDAA and AKC both offer titles to winning dogs, although the exercises and requirements of the two organizations differ.

Agility trials are a great way to keep your dog active, and they will keep you running, too! You should join a local agility club to learn more about the sport.

Tracking

Tracking tests are exciting ways to test your Australian Terrier's instinctive scenting ability on a

Bending his long body, this Australian Terrier enthusiastically approaches the weave pole obstacle at an agility trial.

competitive level. All dogs have a nose, and all breeds are welcome in tracking tests. The first AKC-licensed tracking test took place in 1937 as part of the Utility level at an obedience trial, and thus competitive tracking was officially begun. The first title, Tracking Dog (TD), was offered in 1947, ten years after the first official tracking test. It was not until 1980 that the AKC added the title Tracking Dog Excellent (TDX), which was followed by the title Versatile Surface Tracking (VST) in 1995. Champion Tracker (CT) is awarded to a dog who has earned all three of those titles.

Despite the Australian Terrier's small stature, the breed can be trained to clear short hurdles without difficulty.

Earthdog Events

Earthdog trials are held for those breeds that were developed to "go to ground." These dogs were bred to go down into badger and fox holes and bring out the quarry. Aside from your Australian Terrier, breeds such as Parson Russell Terriers, Dachshunds and other short-legged hunters are used in this fashion. Earthdog trials test the dog in a simulated hunting situation in which trenches are dug and lined, usually with wood. The scent of a rat is laid in the trench, and the quarry is a caged rat at the end of the tunnel. The dog can see and smell the rat but cannot touch or harm the quarry in any way.

There are four levels in earthdog trials. The first, Introduction to Quarry, is for beginners and uses a 10-foot tunnel. No title is awarded at this level. The Junior Earthdog (JE) title is awarded at the next level, which uses a 30-foot tunnel with three 90-degree turns. Two qualifying JE runs are required for a dog to earn the title. The next level, Senior Earthdog (SE), uses the same length tunnel and number of turns as in the JE level, but also has a false den and exit and requires the dog to come out of the tunnel when called. To try for the SE title, a dog must have at least his JE; the SE title requires three qualifying runs at this level. The most difficult of the earthdog tests, Master Earthdog (ME), again uses the 30-foot tunnel with three 90-degree turns, with a false entrance, exit and den. The dog is required to enter in the right place and, in this test, honor another working dog. The ME title requires four qualifying runs, and a dog must have earned his SE title to attempt the ME level.

INDEX

*Page numbers in **boldface** indicate illustrations.*

My Australian Terrier

PUT YOUR PUPPY'S FIRST PICTURE HERE

Dog's Name ______________________________

Date ______________ Photographer ______________________________